Double Black Diamonds
BL Maxwell

Copyright

Double Black Diamonds

BL Maxwell

Editing Provided by AnEdit

Proofreaders: Anita Ford and Nicole Walker

Copyright ©2020 BL Maxwell

ALL RIGHTS RESERVED.

This book may not be reproduced, scanned, or distributed in any printed or electronic form without permissions from the author, except for using small quotes for book review quotations. All characters and storylines are the property of the author. The characters, events and places portrayed in this book are fictitious. Any similarity to real persons, living or dead, is coincidental and not intended by the author.

Trademarks:

This book identifies product names and services known to be trademarks, registered trademarks, or service marks of their respective holders. The author acknowledges the trademarked status and trademark owners of all products referenced in this work of fiction. The publication and use of these trademarks in not authorized, associated with, or sponsored by the trademark owners.

Warning

Intended for a mature an 18+ audience only. This book contains material that may be offensive to some and is intended for a mature, adult audience. It contains graphic language, explicit sexual content, and adult situations.

Epigraph

To TAKING A CHANCE even if it means you could end up with a broken leg.

One
Deschutes

"Come on, man, it'll be fun. It's not that hard and you can handle it no problem."

"I don't know, Dave, I'm fine staying on the blue runs, but I'm not sure I can handle a black run let alone double black diamonds."

Dave and I had been friends for years, but there were many times he'd gotten me in way over my head. He had no fear, where I was more cautious. We had both grown up in Sacramento and every winter we skied a few days of every ski season. But we were far from experts. Dave was just crazy enough to make it *look* like he knew what he was doing.

"Jordan, we came all the way to Park City to check out the skiing. Do you really want to go back home and tell them you didn't want to try Deschutes run?"

I didn't actually know who he meant by "them" and I didn't give a fuck what anyone thought. But dammit, Dave had a way of talking me into trying things I didn't really want to. I scraped the ice off my goggles with my thumb squeegee and tapped my poles together.

The lift ride to the top didn't make the run seem all that intimidating, but when I slid off the seat and stood at the edge of what was clearly marked as a double black diamond run, I knew I was screwed. My mind raced, trying to figure out how I could get back to the bottom without actually skiing this run—and hoped maybe there was an easier way down.

I looked over at Dave. He was tall, thin, and deceptively athletic. His long, light brown hair stuck out from under his knit hat that was tucked under his helmet, and he leaned forward on his skis and moved his legs back and forth, carving two furrows in the soft snow.

"Fuck, okay fine. I'll try. But I swear to god, Dave, you better not leave me there if I have a hard time of it."

He barely gave me a look before he reached out with his poles and exploded down the hill. I watched from the top as he made his way around a few trees in deep snow and even though he was too far forward on his skis, he still managed to make it to the next bend and out of my line of sight.

"Well, here goes nothing." I pushed off and immediately noticed it was a lot steeper than it looked. I tried to keep my edges parallel to the mountain, but it was so steep, and the snow was even deeper than I realized, I was having a hard time staying in control. Fear made me revert back to the wedge I'd learned when I first started skiing so I put my ski tips together and hoped that slowed me down.

And then it happened. I caught the edge of my ski and fell forward over my skis. It was so steep I tumbled a few times and felt a snap in my leg before coming to a stop. One of my skis detached but the other stayed on, twisting my leg at an angle it shouldn't be able to be in. Yep, that was gonna leave a mark.

I tried to right myself enough to sit up, but with the deep snow and being twisted around, I struggled to free myself. Listening for a moment, I hoped for the sound of another skier coming toward me. But all I heard was silence, and the occasional plop of snow dropping off a tree branch. My phone was zipped in the inner chest pocket of my jacket, so I wiggled around until I could take my glove off and pulled it out.

"Please let there be a signal." Swiping it to life, I pressed the emergency option and hoped someone answered. With my helmet on I had to strain to hear, but finally I heard someone speak.

"Emergency services, how can I help you?"

"I'm stuck at the top of Deschutes at Park City ski area." I heard her tapping on a keyboard as she asked me a multitude of questions.

"Sir, do you think you could make it to the top of a trailhead?"

"No, I'm pretty sure my leg is either sprained or broken. I'm stuck in this position and with my leg twisted like it is, I can't get up." A shiver ran through me, as the cold of the snow seeped into me through my ski clothes.

"Are you in danger of hypothermia?"

"I—I'm not sure. I can't move and I'm planted in the snow."

"Okay, sir, please hold."

My hand started to shake, and my teeth chattered as I smashed the phone to my ear so I wouldn't miss anything she said.

"Sorry about that, I've called the ski area, and they're dispatching ski patrol to assist you. You'll want to listen for a snowmobile. I've relayed to them that you're injured and may not be able to ski down."

"Th—thank you. I'm getting really cold."

"Try to pull your hands inside your jacket and close to your body. Since we don't know what's happened to your leg, I'd advise you to not move it until you know for sure if it's broken."

"I'll try." I pulled one arm in, then passed my phone to that hand and pulled in the other. Hugging my arms around my waist I tried like hell to feel some warmth, and I hoped help arrived soon. Just as snow started to lightly fall.

Two
Meat Wagon

"Trace Griffin," I answered the emergency call like I did every time my radio crackled to life.

"Hey, Trace. There's a skier stuck at the top of Deschutes. He thinks he has a broken leg. You better take the meat wagon and head up there."

"Sure thing, Lance. I'll take Brad with me."

"Roger that, and, Trace, watch it, there's a front moving in. Don't waste any time."

"Got it, I'll leave now."

I walked over to where the other ski patrollers were gathered waiting to find out where they'd be sent to next.

"Brad, you're with me." He grabbed his skis and we both hurried to a snowmobile.

"What's going on?" he asked. He was one of the newbies this year, but at twenty-eight he wasn't one of the youngest. And his medical experience and skiing ability were both what helped him land the job. His dark hair and dark eyes didn't hurt either as far as I was concerned.

"Skier stuck at the top of Deschutes, possible broken leg." I started the snowmobile and waited for him to attach a sled and stow his skis. He jumped on the back and patted my shoulder when he was ready. I didn't hesitate as I took off for the nearest logging road that would lead to the top of the mountain.

It was slow going. It had been snowing off and on the past few days leaving a new layer of fresh snow. Even though the snow here in Utah was dry and light, it was still enough to give us trouble when it started to pile up.

"How much longer do you think it'll take us?" Brad shouted, leaning in close so I could hear over the machine.

"Shouldn't be too much longer," I answered just as we crested the hill that would lead us to where Deschutes started. I waved at the lift operator and was past him before he had time to react. Staying to the side of the trail, I avoided the skiers and boarders that were just getting off the lift and bent over tightening their boots before picking a trail to ride.

We stopped at the top and Brad hopped off and clicked on his skis; after stomping a few times he nodded he was ready. I led the way down and he followed behind the basket. There were no other skiers on the trail, so I let it slide as fast as it wanted to and wove between the trees. The snow was really starting to stick up here covering any fresh tracks.

Brad skied to the left of me and rounded a bend. A stand of Aspen partially obscured my view of the trail, and just as I slid out in the turn, I saw his ski sticking out of the snow and slowed as fast as I could. Brad made a sweeping turn and stopped parallel to the slope.

"Here."

A hand appeared out of the snow, and I realized I wouldn't have seen him if I hadn't spotted his ski. He stuck his hand up from where the snow had completely covered him in the time it took us to get there.

I hopped off the snowmobile and ran over to him. Brushing the snow off I found him curled in a ball. His gloved hand was sticking out of the top of his jacket, he still had his helmet and goggles on, but his lips were blue from the cold.

"We're here, can you move?" He shook his head and his teeth chattered as he pulled his hand back into his jacket. "Don't worry, we'll get you out of here." He nodded and tried to curl up more. I brushed the snow off him as Brad pulled an emergency kit off the snowmobile.

"Brad, help me straighten his leg out so we can get him onto the sled." We worked fast and tried not to hurt him any more than we had to as we flipped him around to untangle his legs. Once the remaining ski was off it made it much easier to straighten his legs out.

"I shouldn't have been on this run. It was too advanced." He grimaced in pain as he spoke.

"It's okay, we'll worry about that once we get you down the hill." He winced as I squeezed his leg checking for a break.

"Is that tender?"

"Yeah, I heard something snap when I fell."

"Brad, help me lift him onto the basket." Brad hurried to slide it closer to where the skier lay, and between the two of us we quickly had him secured on the back of it. I strapped a warming blanket around him and decided to leave his ski boot on until we were at the bottom of the hill.

"Brad's going to ski behind us and keep the basket steady. Don't worry, we'll be at the bottom in no time." He reached his hand out and raised his goggles so I could finally see his eyes. They were a clear green and any other day I probably wouldn't have noticed, but his cheeks were red from the cold and the contrast made his eyes stand out so clear. I shook my head to focus back on getting him down.

"Thank you for finding me. I wasn't sure what would happen if I was there too much longer."

I patted his shoulder and wrapped the blanket a little tighter around him. "Just doing my job. Let's get you down below so we can check out that leg."

He ducked down under the blanket without another word as we made our way down the mountain. All the way there I thought of his eyes and wondered if he was here alone or if he'd come with someone else. I'd find out soon enough as we were nearly at the hut. We slid to a stop, and I jumped off to hurry him inside to the warm.

"Is he okay?" a guy asked as he skied up next to us.

"We'll know in a few minutes." Guess he wasn't alone after all. I wasn't willing to think too hard on why that thought made my heart hurt a little in disappointment.

"Come on, let's get you inside," I said as I unhooked the sled from the back of the snowmobile and waited for Brad to help me.

Three
Bad Break

I TRIED NOT TO think about how fast we were moving when the ski patrol brought me down in the basket. We'd joked for years calling it the meat wagon, and right now I was the meat. I just hoped I didn't end up wrapped around a tree in some freak mishap on the way down.

At the bottom of the mountain when we came to a stop, I heard voices, but with my helmet on and wrapped in a blanket, I couldn't hear who it was or what they were saying. I was carried into a building, and the heat hit me like a wall. I tried to push the blanket off, but someone pressed it back down.

"Give us just a second, I know it's hot in here."

They set me down on the floor and finally unwrapped the blanket. My eyes locked with the same guy who'd helped me at the top of the mountain. Those intense blue eyes were all business, as he and another man lifted me from the basket onto an exam table.

"What are his injuries?" a woman asked as she walked over and started examining me.

"I think my leg is broken," I gritted out; now that I was warming up the pain cut me like a hot knife.

"Easy there," the guy with the eyes said. "It was twisted up behind him and his ski didn't detach. I'm not sure it's broken, but I didn't want to remove his boot just in case."

"Good call," she said and started unclasping my ski boot. "I'm Jenny Nolan. I'm going to assess your injuries and see if we need to send you to the medical center." When the last clasp was unlatched and she pulled the front of the boot out to open it up, the pain hit a whole new level and I worried I'd either pass out or throw up.

"He doesn't look so good. You might need to give him something for pain."

I nodded my head, and at the same time the man unclasped my helmet and slipped it and my goggles off. His eyes met mine and even through the pain I couldn't help but notice how hot he was. Fuck's sake, I was in a ski patrol hut, I needed to get it together.

"What's your name?" he asked. "I didn't take the time to ask when we were on the hill."

I loosened my jaw that was clenched in pain as she pulled my boot off. "Fuck!"

"Your name is fuck?"

I was in pain, but I didn't miss the humor in his voice. He was handsome, alarmingly so. With dark hair cut close on the sides, and blue eyes so clear I couldn't look away.

"Sorry, no, my name is Jordan, Jordan James."

"Well, Jordan James, I'm Trace Griffin, and as soon as Jenny makes sure you're stable we're going to take you to the medical center downtown for an x-ray."

The woman, Jenny, asked me a lot of questions about allergies, pre-existing conditions, and assessed my pain level. She explained she was a doctor, and she helped ski patrol guy with my jacket and pulled my sweater down enough to stick a needle in my arm. Warmth spread through my body.

"That's just something for the pain. I'm still not sure it's broken, but there's no need for you to be so uncomfortable. That'll relax you until we know for sure what's going on."

I nodded and closed my eyes as the warmth began to spread.

"Jordan? Oh my god, I am so sorry. I didn't know you were hurt. I thought you were just taking your time."

"Wait, you can't be in here," someone said to Dave.

"It's okay, this is the asshole that thought it was a good idea for me to try to ski a double black diamond," I mumbled without even bothering to open my eyes.

"Oh really?" the hot guy said. The silence was deafening, and I wanted to know what was going on, but sleep claimed me.

Four
A Good Break

As a member of the ski patrol at Park City, I felt responsible for every person I brought down the mountain. But something roared to life in me when I realized Jordan's friend had not only encouraged him to go down a run that was, from what I picked up, way too advanced for him, but he'd left him there and not checked to make sure he'd come down.

"I'm really sorry, Jordan. I should have made sure you were okay."

"It's okay, Dave," Jordan said, as Jenny fitted his leg with a brace so he wasn't injured more on the way to get an x-ray.

"You got lucky; it doesn't look like you have any injuries other than your leg. Although if you had been out there much longer you could have gone into hypothermia, but lucky enough you were able to call for help," Jenny said as she helped him sit up. "Trace, would you mind driving him to the medical center.

"I can take him. I mean, we don't have a car but I can call for a ride to take him." His friend jumped around on his toes and tried everything to get us to agree. But that wasn't going to happen.

"Don't worry about it. I can take him in my truck. Would that be okay with you?" I turned and met Jordan's eyes. He was pretty out of it from the pain meds, so his eyes were a little glassy and a lot droopy.

"Yeah, that would be great. Don't worry, Dave, you go ahead and ski. I'll meet you back at the room later."

"Are you sure? I feel awful that you got hurt."

"Don't worry, you'll make it up to me by buying me dinner." Jordan's eyes slid shut as he spoke, and I knew he'd be asleep in no time.

"Okay, I think we need to get you going. We have a wheelchair we can use to take you to the truck." I didn't wait for him to answer, just walked over to it and brought it back to him.

"I don't need that," he said, and tried to stand.

"Don't even think about it. Let me help you." I lifted him off the table and set him into the chair before he had a chance to answer, but he didn't fight it.

"Thank you," he mumbled as I turned to leave the room.

"Jordan, I'm really sorry," his friend said again as he clomped along next to the chair in his ski boots.

Jordan raised his hand and waved him off. "See you later, Dave."

At my truck I opened the door and lifted him onto the passenger seat. I made sure his leg was tucked in safely before I reached over him and fastened his seatbelt. He opened his eyes as I threw a blanket over him, and we were so close I could see all the shades of green reflected in them.

I stepped back and shut his door. *What the hell was that all about*? I tried to remember the last time I'd noticed someone's eyes or noticed anything that didn't have to do with work. I was in the driver's seat before I had time to answer my own question.

"Don't worry, it won't take long, it's just down the road."

"S'ok. I'm so tired, whatever she gave me really knocked me out."

"If she hadn't given it to you, you'd be in a lot of pain. I know Jenny didn't want to confirm it, but I'll be surprised if your leg isn't broken. You really wrenched it." I glanced at him as I talked and noticed he'd started to lean in the seat a little. There was no reason for more conversation, he was out of it.

Within a few minutes we bounced into the parking lot. The constant light snow kept the snowplows busy. The entrance was clear, but the parking lot was surrounded by a mound of snow that would grow higher and higher after every plowing. I pulled up to the door to make it easier to get him inside, and as I came to a stop, he slumped closer to me. He really was cute, and he had a broken leg I reminded myself.

I walked around to the passenger side, and as I opened the door, Lissa, one of the nurses, rushed out with a wheelchair.

"Hey, Trace, Brad called ahead and gave me his information. We've got a room ready for him." She tipped her chin toward Jordan as I set him in the chair.

"He wasn't out there long but he was pretty cold when we found him. His leg was wrenched behind him because his binding didn't release."

"Okay, I've got it from here," she said, and started to push him into the medical center.

He hadn't woken up and was still bundled up in the blanket. As soon as they crossed the threshold of the entrance, it was as though an invisible thread pulled me toward him. I was already through the door before I realized what I was doing.

"Trace? Did you need something?"

"No, I just think I should stay with him. He's not from here, and his friend is still on the mountain."

"Okay, but don't be surprised if we put you to work."

"I'm fine with that," I said, and followed them to an exam room.

"You can help me with the x-ray since he's still asleep." Lissa rushed around the room and gathered everything she'd need. "I'll need to take off his ski clothes. Can you give me a hand?"

"Sure." I slid his jacket off one arm and tucked the blanket back around him. He still hadn't woken up or reacted at all. "Jenny gave him something for pain, but he's been out on and off since she gave it to him."

"He might be sensitive to pain meds. Better to be out of it than deal with that pain. I really only need his pants off for the x-ray, so his ski pants have to go. You can leave his shirt."

Lissa helped as we took off his other ski boot and I unzipped the sides of his ski pants and tried to pull them off over the splint we'd put on him. He had thermals on under his ski pants, but we were able to move them up his leg enough that we didn't need to cut them.

"That should do it." She pulled the x-ray machine over from where it was on a metal bracket attached to the wall. Lissa positioned his leg after I showed her where I thought he'd injured it. After stepping in and out of the room a few times, and changing the position of his leg, she said she had all she needed and walked out the door leaving me alone with Jordan.

"Trace, what's going on?" Drake Flynn walked into the room like he always did. Like he owned it and you were lucky he didn't make you leave to make room for his ego.

"Not much, just making sure this guy's leg isn't hurt more than we suspected."

"And by 'we' you mean that little pack of wannabe paramedics you work with?"

I crossed my arms and kept my mouth shut. He could fuck off. I asked myself for the millionth time *why* I'd ever dated him. Fuck my life.

Five
Ski Patrol Guy

I woke up and for a second, I thought I was asleep at the hotel, but then I heard someone talking in the room. It didn't sound like Dave, and I didn't think he'd bring someone back to the room we were sharing. But stranger things had happened.

"Dave?" Rustling next to me caught my attention and I opened my eyes to see who was there.

"No, your friend stayed at Park City. Well, I didn't actually give him a choice." Those eyes . . . I knew those eyes.

"Ski patrol guy," I said, when I finally made the connection.

"Yes, my name is Trace, but I answer to ski patrol guy too." He gave me a warm smile and I felt myself smile back before I had time to even think about it.

"Oh boy, next one on the hook already?" another guy asked from the other side of the room.

Ski patrol guy didn't bother to even look in the direction of the other guy's voice. His eyes, those intense blue eyes, never left mine.

"How are you feeling? You took a pretty bad fall out there."

"I'm not sure, I don't remember much after you picked me up and brought me back down the hill."

"We gave you something for pain. Turns out you do have a broken leg. Nothing too serious—"

"Ahem, how about you let the actual medical professional tell him this part?" the other guy said and stepped in front of Trace with his hand out. "Jordan James, I'm Doctor Flynn."

I looked between him and ski patrol guy—Trace—and tried to put some order to these two strangers. There was a weird vibe in the room that if I wasn't mistaken, was the distinctive feeling of two exes trying to play nice. I realized I still hadn't taken his hand, so I did slowly and shook it.

"Is my leg broken?"

"Yes, you fractured your tibia, just at the boot-line. You'll have a boot until the swelling goes down then you'll need a cast. I'll need to see you back here in a week—"

"Oh, I won't be here that long. I return to Sacramento in a few days."

"I can check it out before you leave then. When you get home be sure you call your regular doctor and have him examine your leg and set you up with a cast. Not that he can tell you anything different than I've told you." He mumbled that last bit under his breath and turned to glance at ski patrol guy.

"So boot then cast, right. It's going to suck that I'm on a ski vacation and can't ski."

"Let me go and organize the boot, I'll be right back." He walked out of the room without another word as Trace shook his head.

"An ex?" I asked; apparently, I'd lost my filter along with my dignity when I landed ass over teakettle on that run.

"Yep, sooo much ex."

"He seems really . . . nice?"

His eyes met mine for a split second before he folded in half in silent laughter. When he straightened back up his face was bright red with the effort of controlling that laugh. "Sorry, sorry," he choked out. "It's just that he's such a cocky asshole. And not the fun kind of cocky at all."

"Did you mean to say all that?"

"Not really, he just pisses me off and annoys the hell out of me. It makes me lose my train of thought."

"Yeah, I kinda noticed."

The door opened and Doctor Flynn walked in followed by a nurse.

"Lissa will help you with the boot, you'll want to loosen it every few hours and ice your leg to assist with the swelling. You'll also need to keep all weight off it for now until you get the cast."

The nurse assisted the ex and finally I was ready to leave. I'd pulled my ski pants back on and they left the bottom of the leg unzipped, they actually fit better over the boot than my jeans would have.

"Can you call a ride for me?" I turned to look at Trace.

"I can take you to your hotel." He hadn't taken his eyes off my leg as he said it, so when I nodded, I wasn't sure he knew I'd answered. But when he helped me up and into the wheelchair, I went along with him.

He wheeled me to the entrance and we both looked at the snow that was now coming down so heavy I realized there was no way he could push the wheelchair through it to his truck.

"Wait right here, I'll bring the truck over." Before I could answer, he was jogging away pulling his hood over his head.

And I wondered one more time what the fuck I was doing.

Six

Exes, Boots, and Dinner

"Where are you staying?" I asked as I pulled slowly out of the parking lot and onto the main road.

"We're at a small hotel in the center of town. Close to the town lift."

"The Chateau Apres Lodge? Good choice."

"It's pretty basic, but we thought we'd be out skiing all day, so we didn't want to spend a lot on the hotel."

"You and your boyfriend?" I attempted to sound nonchalant but the look he gave me told me he saw right through me.

"Dave? Oh my god no. He's a ladies' man, or he thinks he is anyway." He laughed. "If you only knew all the times he thought he was so slick, but not so much. He's a nice enough guy, but, well, he's a little clueless sometimes."

"So, how did you two end up on Deschutes?" I asked, not taking my eyes off the road.

"Dave said it was easier than it was rated. I knew I was in trouble as soon as I started downhill. I tried to slide and keep my skis parallel to the hill, but the trail was too narrow. When I tried to snowplow, everything went to shit."

He did what? "You tried to snowplow down Deschutes?"

"Well yeah. It was too steep, too narrow, and there was too much powder. I couldn't handle it. Dave took off and was gone before I was even over the ridge and on the trail. Dick."

"I hope he realizes you really could have gotten in trouble. Good thing you were able to call for help. Hard to say when someone would have found you."

"He realizes. He was scared. I know he'd never do anything to hurt me on purpose. He's just very impulsive. All he was thinking about was he was finally on a run he'd seen in ski videos. He imagines himself to be an excellent skier when really, he has no fear. He just dives right in and lets it rip."

"He did look a little freaked out. I have to admit I tried to play it up a little, so he knew it was serious." I smiled at him; his friend was worried it had been easy to see. But he'd still been irresponsible. "Here's your place. Did you guys ride the town lift up to Park City today?"

"Yeah, you can just drop me off out front. I can make it to my room on my own."

I parked the truck and shut the motor off. "There is no way in hell you can make it to your room on your own. You can't put any weight on that foot. I was going to get you some crutches, but until you have them you won't be able to get around."

"Oh, I hadn't thought of that."

"You can stay with me. I'm off the next week—this was my last shift. I can go get whatever you need to take with you." I couldn't seem to stop the words from spilling out of my mouth. I hadn't planned to take him home with me. This was supposed to be my week of being lazy at home. Late nights reading in front of the fire, working in my workshop, and binging on Netflix. Maybe he wouldn't take me up on it?

I opened the door slightly and waited for his reaction. "I can't do that. What would Dave do? I'd be deserting him."

"Why don't we go to your room and you can call him . . . if he's okay with it, then we can just grab your things and get to my place before the snow gets too deep."

"You'd do that? Let me stay there on your week off?"

I shrugged. "Sure, it's not like I couldn't fight you off if you tried anything funny. Are you going to try something funny?"

"What are you talking about? I couldn't do something funny if I wanted to."

"Okay then, let's go get your shit." I walked around to his side and opened the door. Without thinking I reached across him, unbuckled his seatbelt, and lifted him into my arms. "How's your leg feeling? You're probably going to be ready for a pain med soon." Having him this close was distracting. His eyes had been what had drawn me in, but the perfect angles of his face, the way his brows arched in reaction to every comment, intrigued me even more.

"I don't do so well with them, they knock me out."

"That explains why you were so out of it when we got to the medical center. I thought maybe it was all too much for you." I tipped my chin at the guy at the front desk when he waved a hello toward us, and he didn't question why I was walking in carrying one of their guests.

"What room are you in?"

"Room 220. Maybe I could ask for a room on the first floor?"

"The first floor is a youth hostel. Unless you're willing to share your room with a few more fellow skiers I wouldn't recommend it." I took the stairs and carried him up without much effort.

"Do you mind if we get those crutches? I feel awful that you're having to carry me all over."

I turned down the hall and, in a few steps, we were at his door. He fished the keycard out of his jacket pocket, and between us we opened the door and moved inside.

"If you can put me down, I can tell you where my things are. Most of it's still in my suitcase."

I picked up the suitcase he indicated and walked around the room gathering up a few pieces of clothing, toiletries, and his phone charger. He was focused on his phone and wasn't paying too much attention to what I was grabbing.

"Is there anything else?" I scanned the room, but I didn't know what things were his or his friend's.

"My toothbrush. I think that's all. Are you sure you don't mind? I really can stay here on my own."

"Oh really? What happens when you have to go to the bathroom?"

The wide-eyed look he gave me said it all. He was fucked if he didn't have someone to help him the next few days at least.

"Don't worry, Jordan, I'm not about to leave you to figure it out on your own. Now tell me if there's anything else you need while we're here?"

He looked around one more time from where he sat on the bed. "No, I think that's it. I'm going to leave a note for Dave in case he doesn't get the text I sent. I still haven't heard back from him."

I handed him a hotel scratchpad and he wrote his message then tossed it onto the other bed.

"That should do it. If there's anything else I need I can have Dave bring it to me. Oh, what's your address so I can leave him that information."

"Sure." I rattled off my address and after I handed him the pad of paper, he wrote it down. "Stay right here and I'll take your things down and come back to get you."

I jogged down the stairs and the guy at the front desk once again waved like I did this every day. The snow had picked up and was really sticking. No doubt by tomorrow we'd be stuck at my place until the plow could get to us. I made a mental note to stop for some crutches on the way home. I put his things behind the seat and hurried back inside. The sooner we were out of the snow the better.

Seven
Ski Patrol Guy's House

I SAT ON MY bed and tried to ignore the growing throb of pain in my leg. What the hell was I doing trusting this stranger? I guess the fact he worked for ski patrol had something to do it. But really, I didn't know anything about him. And where the hell was Dave? That asshole.

The door opened and Trace walked in. "You ready to go?"

"Yeah, you're really sure about this?" He smiled at me then, and everything about his face changed. His eyes were bright with humor and was that a dimple? Oh, dear lord. I swallowed with a gulp. I was so in trouble with ski patrol guy.

"Jordan, if I wasn't sure I wouldn't have offered. Now come on, let's get you down to my truck. It's starting to build up out there and I wanted to get your crutches on the way."

"Crutches in snow, sounds fun." He lifted me up and chuckled at that.

"Once we get home we'll stay there until the weather breaks. It's supposed to snow at least the next couple of days."

"Do you want to stop and get some groceries or anything? I hate to use all your stuff."

"Don't worry about it, I've been squirreling away supplies for months. I learned that lesson the hard way when I first moved here."

"Okay but I'm going to pitch in for food or drinks or something. I can't let you pay for everything."

"Let's just worry about getting to my house first." He rushed out the entrance of the hotel and I realized I hadn't even noticed him going back down the stairs. Damn dimple.

I cringed at the snow hitting me in the face as Trace rushed to get me inside his truck. I turned at the wrong time and banged the boot against the door and for two seconds I held my breath to avoid shedding actual tears in front of him.

"Jordan? Are you okay?"

I cracked my eyes open to find him closer than I expected, and his face strained with worry.

"Yep, just fine." He helped me adjust my leg so the boot fit better in the truck. Fucking boot. My teeth were clenched so tight I worried I'd need to find a dentist next and rolled my eyes at myself.

"Don't move, my house is really close." Without another word he shut the door and hurried around to the driver's side.

"How much snow is expected?" I looked out at the steady snowfall that had only picked up in intensity as we sat there.

"Not sure, they told us this morning there was a front moving in, but I didn't hear how much they were expecting."

He reversed out of the space and we made our way down the street in front of the hotel toward the downtown area of Park City. "How do you like living here?"

"I like it a lot. The snow can be a lot some winters. But it's beautiful here, and I like that even though it's a busy place, it's still got that small town feel to it. What do you do back in Sacramento?"

"I'm a mechanic. Dave and I work at a place in downtown. We've been there since we graduated high school."

"You two must be pretty good friends if you work together and go on vacation together."

"Yeah, we get along. He's a handful though. He's a great mechanic, but with everything else he doesn't look before he leaps. We both had the week after Christmas off, and he thought it was a great time to check out Park City. I had no other plans so it sounded good to me."

We bumped along a side road that went behind the businesses lining the main street, until we pulled up to a small cabin. Christmas lights were strung on every part of the front of the A-frame shaped building.

"Wow, this is amazing."

"Wait til you see it at night." He grinned and once again that elusive dimple made its appearance. "I know the holidays are over, but I enjoy the lights. And if people don't like it, they can fuck off."

I nodded my agreement as I took in all the wires and shapes that I knew would be beautiful at dark, and maybe when it wasn't snowing so hard.

"I'm sorry, I was so focused on driving in the snow, I forgot to stop and get you some crutches. I'll get you settled inside and drive over to get them."

"You don't mind me being here alone?"

"You don't mind being here alone?" he shot back with a grin.

"Nope, I'm ready for a pain pill and a nap."

He once again carried me from the truck and balanced me as he opened his door. "Welcome to my home." He set me down on a couch that was way more comfy than the bed at the hotel.

The A-frame shape created a loft at the top of the house, and the open floor plan meant every room was easy to see from where I sat. The kitchen was rustic but clean and the stainless-steel appliances gave it a bit of a modern look.

The interior walls were a warm wood with lots of red, black, and green sprinkled in all over the place. The fireplace at the center of the room had a hearth made of red brick with a woodstove insert, and a wide mantle painted bright white.

"Wow, this is nice. It's very cozy."

"Why thank you. I was trying to create a sanctuary from the outside world. When I'm not at work I'm more than happy to hibernate at home."

"I wouldn't mind hibernating here," I murmured without thinking about it. His house was so inviting and homey. I wouldn't mind staying here at all.

Eight
Favorite Things

I hurried back to the medical center and hoped I didn't run into Drake again, once a month was too much. When we'd first met, I thought he was fun to hang out with, but I soon realized his sarcasm was always on full display, and he liked to think that he was just a little better than most people he met.

There was no sign of his car as I pulled into the parking lot and I hoped like hell my luck held out. I stopped as close as I could to the entrance and hopped over the mounds of snow that now dotted the parking lot.

"Hey, Trace, I thought you might be back." Lissa walked into the front exam room and returned with a set of crutches.

"Thanks, he's not going to be able to get around at all without these."

"I'm sure you could help him out," she said with a grin I tried not to return but couldn't help myself.

I rubbed the back of my neck and looked down at the floor. "He's a nice guy. I felt bad, his friend took him down a run he couldn't handle and didn't check to make sure he was following him. I just couldn't leave him at a hotel where he'd be sitting in his room all alone." And why the hell was I telling her this?

"Good for you, Trace, you deserve to have some fun too you know." She patted me on the arm as she handed me the crutches with a warm smile.

"Yeah, I have the next week off, so I'll be staying close to home anyway."

"Lucky you. They just upgraded this storm so don't be surprised if you end up stuck there a few days."

"How much snow are they predicting? I hadn't heard when I was at work earlier."

"I heard at least eighteen. Just be sure you have everything you need while you're out, so you don't have to stress leaving during the storm. It's supposed to be here a few days at least."

"Thanks, Lissa, I appreciate your advice." I took the crutches from her and waved as I walked out the door. The snow was heavier still, and I jogged back to my truck and put the crutches behind the seat. I realized then I hadn't given Jordan his suitcase, and I hoped there was nothing he needed too urgently. Then I remembered he couldn't walk. If he needed to go to the bathroom or get a drink he was stuck on my couch. "Fuck, why didn't I think of that earlier."

I rushed home as much as I could in the heavy snow and hurried inside with the crutches and his belongings. "Jordan, I'm so sorry—"

He was on the couch where I'd left him, but he'd pulled a throw over himself and was lying down with his leg resting on a few pillows. The day and his pain meds had finally caught up with him. I took a few seconds to really take him in. He was cute, and now that I could see his hands, the fact that he was a mechanic was a little more obvious with the visible nicks and calluses.

His dark hair was longer than I thought, and in sleep he looked more relaxed than I'd seen him other than when he was passed out earlier. I finally pulled my eyes away from him and set his belongings and the crutches next to where he slept.

Might as well stop wasting time and start making dinner. I decided soup would be a good idea on this cold day, so I got busy getting all the ingredients together for a hearty pasta fagioli then since I needed to stay busy a while longer, I decided I had time to make some home-baked bread. Luckily, I kept a starter handy for just such occasions. Well not really an occasion, I just needed a reason to bake a loaf of bread and I was on it.

It didn't take me long to make a couple of round loaves that would be prefect for bread bowls. I was about to take them out of the oven when a noise behind me caught my attention.

"Hey," Jordan croaked out. He stood on the other side of the kitchen island balancing on his uninjured leg and one crutch. "Can I get something to drink?"

"Fuck, I'm sorry. I meant to put a glass of water next to you. What do you want? I have pretty much anything." I hurried to the fridge and swung open the door. He slowly made his way to it and chose a soda. "How are you feeling?"

"Like a truck hit me. I think they were right to give me the pain meds. I thought it was overkill at first."

"Are you in pain? Here, let me help you back to the couch."

"Do you mind if I sit at the island? I'd rather see what you're up to in here. It smells amazing."

"Thanks. I made soup and fresh baked bread. Oh, I almost forgot." I turned to take the bread out of the oven, and the crispy brown crust told me I'd done it just in time.

"Wow I'm impressed. Handsome and can cook," he said with a smile.

"Well you might change your mind when you actually taste it." I had to admit it was nice to have someone to cook for.

"I doubt that," he mumbled, and wiggled around on one of the stools trying to get comfortable. "Have you always cooked?"

"Nope, when I moved here the winters were a big influence. Like I said, you never know how long you'll be stuck. Binge watching Netflix gets old after a few weeks. Although I have been inspired by a few of the baking shows." I cut the centers out of the loaves and filled them with soup before adding parmesan cheese. I set a plate in front of Jordan and his eyes widened.

"You made all this?"

"Yes, I promise I didn't stop on the way home and get takeout then throw it in the oven to make it look like I cooked it." I smiled at that thought, I knew I could cook a meal better than any takeout. Well I liked to think I could.

Jordan leaned forward and inhaled. "Thank you so much. I haven't had a home cooked meal in so long."

"Well dig in, I want to know what you think." My eyes were drawn to his lips as he took a spoonful of soup and blew to cool it. And why was I noticing his lips? The groan he let out when he tasted it didn't help either, but it did make me happy that he enjoyed my cooking. His eyes met mine and I realized I was still staring and hadn't touched my soup yet.

He patted the stool next to him. "Trace, come here and try this, it's so good." His smile was probably the last sign I needed to know for sure he was someone I was not going to mind being stuck with.

Nine
A Cozy Fire

I ate another bowl of the soup Trace had made. "My stomach feels like it's about to burst but I want to eat more. It's so good."

"Well thank you. I don't get to cook for someone else very often."

"Did you cook for that guy at the medical center?" I shouldn't have asked, but I couldn't seem to stop myself.

"Drake? Yes sadly."

"I smell a story, did he not like your cooking?"

"Oh god, you're going to make me tell you." His head slumped forward barely missing his bowl.

I laughed at his dramatics, something very different than his professional side I'd seen all day. He was so welcoming, and I felt really comfortable around him, even though we were strangers. "Tell me. I need some entertainment."

"Well, I met him at the medical center when I first moved here. I thought he would be interesting since he's a doctor. But what you see is what you get. He's cocky as fuck and is more than happy to spend hours telling you all about how awesome he is and how lucky you are to be in his presence."

"He didn't."

"Oh, he did, for hours and hours. I invited him here for dinner and he complained about everything I served, how it was not what he was expecting, and how he could recommend some recipes that might help."

My eyes widened at that. The little bit of time I'd watched Trace in the kitchen I knew he was very comfortable there and didn't need any help.

"What a dick."

"Yep, that's what I said as I shoved him out the door. He insulted me for hours then tried to schmooze me. There was no way in hell I was falling for that."

"Wow, I can see him doing that. I mean, I don't know him, but he came off as a know-it-all."

"So, tell me about your friend."

He changed the subject so fast it took me a minute to recover. "Oh Dave? We just work together. Don't worry, we've never dated, thank god. He's a mess as far as dating goes. And like I said before he's straight. I'm sort of surprised I haven't heard from him yet."

"Does he do that often?"

"What? Take me down a run and leave me with a broken leg? No, that's a first. He has ditched me many times for a cute girl though."

Almost on cue my phone rang from where I'd left it on the couch. I started to try to stand on the crutch, but Trace stopped me. "I'll get it."

He hurried over and handed it to me. I looked at who it was and rolled my eyes. "Hey, Dave, did you finally remember me?"

"Dude, I'm sorry. I met someone and—"

"It's fine, I went to the room and took everything to Trace's place. Go ahead and enjoy the rest of the week. He said he's fine with me hanging out here and he has the time off."

"You're sure? I mean, you don't know that guy."

"Well, he saved my ass when I could have frozen to death at the top of the hill so I'm thinking he's a pretty safe bet."

"Sorry, I really did think you were right behind me."

"Don't worry, I'll make you pay at work. You know all those oil changes you're so fond of? Guess who'll be doing all of mine when we get back." His groan was payment enough for now. "I'm getting five-star treatment here. Trace is an amazing chef, we just finished some soup and home-baked bread. Sorry not sorry you couldn't join us."

"Oh my god, well, enjoy yourself. I'll be eating at—I don't know yet. But I'll be eating alone. The girl I met earlier has to work so we're planning to go ski together tomorrow."

"Have fun, I won't be skiing for a while. Probably not until next season."

"Sorry, man," Dave said again.

"It's all good, and I'll be expecting a season pass next year for the resort of my choosing."

"Sounds good to me. At least I'll know you'll still ski with me. Can't lose my ski buddy."

I glanced at Trace and he shook his head with a grin.

"Right, well, I'm going to go. But we'll get together for dinner or lunch before we're ready to head back to Sacramento." After saying good-bye, I set my phone down on the counter and finished the rest of my soup and bread. "So, what's on the agenda for the rest of the night?"

"Whatever you feel like doing. I have all the streaming channels so we could watch a movie or something. Or I have a bunch of board games if you're into that, or we could do some arts and crafts."

"What kind of arts and crafts?" I asked. Hey, I was more than willing to try whatever it was.

"Well, I've been painting some new lawn characters for the front of the house. Every year I add more to the holiday display, and this year I'm working on a skier made out of wood, that's going down a hill. I'm going to line his path with lights, so it looks like he's in motion." He described it all so well I could imagine it.

"Is he going to be bombing down the slope of your house? Because that would be cool. You could make him look like a ski jumper in the tuck position."

He pointed his finger at me as he spoke. "That's a great idea. I was going to have him skiing across the front of the house, but I love the idea of him racing down the side of the roof."

"Do you make the designs yourself?" I asked; now I was even more intrigued.

"I cut the shapes out of wood then paint them myself. It keeps me busy when I'm not working. I try to always have a project going so I don't get bored."

"What do you do during the summers here?"

"I work as a paramedic for one of the ambulance companies in the area. They really only need extra help during the summer months, so it works out great for me."

"Trace Griffin, you live a very interesting life."

"Nah, I just do what works for me and keeps me busy."

My eyes started to close on their own, and Trace scooped me up and carried me to the couch.

"Get some sleep, I'm going to work on my project."

I fell asleep before I could reply and in my dreams Trace and I flew down double black diamond runs and neither of us fell as we raced each other to the bottom.

Ten

Monopoly

WHAT A DAY THIS had been. When I went to work, I was looking forward to having time off. After the rush of the holidays and with the heavy snowfall we'd had this year it had been a busy season, and it didn't look like that would be changing until spring.

I helped Jordan settle his leg on a few pillows and cleaned up the kitchen. I wasn't sure what had prompted me to ask him to stay, but I was glad I did. Even though it was dark out it was still early. I checked on Jordan again before I slipped my coat on and went out back to my workshop. There were a few projects I'd been working on, but I liked the idea Jordan had come up with.

Sketching out the skier on a sheet of plywood, I double checked that the size was right for him to ski down the roof and checked the angle so his skis would slide down the slope smoothly. I wanted him to be larger than life so he would stand out against the other lights and displays I already had.

When I was happy with his shape and size, I used a jigsaw to roughly cut out the shape before using a sander to shape it. I set down the sander and ran my fingers over the edges feeling for any rough spots or edges that were shaped a little funny. I glanced at my phone and realized I'd been out here a few hours. I wiped my hands off on a shop towel and tossed it on my workbench and turned around—to find Jordan leaning on his crutches in the doorway, watching me.

"Jordan, how'd you get out here?" I rushed over to him and had to stop myself from patting him down for injuries.

"Is this where you work?"

I looked around the shop trying to see it through his eyes. It was a pretty basic woodshop. I didn't have much room for tools or equipment I wouldn't use very often. Our eyes met and for a moment everything around us faded into the background. Fuck. "Yeah," I croaked out, cleared my throat and tried again. "Yeah. This is my hidey-hole. My place to get away from everything and everyone."

"Oh, I'm sorry. I'll wait inside." He shuffled around to go back inside.

I rushed over and gripped his arm. "Jordan, I didn't mean you."

He slowly turned his head and met my eyes again, and before I knew what I was doing, I had him wrapped in my arms and was kissing him. His crutches fell to the ground as he gripped me just as hard. I pressed him back against the door frame forgetting about his injury and jumping back away when I remembered.

"I'm so sorry, did I hurt you?" He tried to balance on his good leg but the boot on his other leg was too heavy and threatened to topple him. I gripped his arms again and he gripped me back.

"Can we do that again?" he asked, his pupils dark and lips pink and swollen.

"Yeah," I croaked out again. "Oh my god, you've got me all twisted up. Let's go inside, I don't want you to hurt yourself."

"Would you help me with my crutches?" he asked.

They were both splayed in different directions on the floor and I didn't want to not be touching him, so I scooped him up in my arms and kicked the door further open.

"Oh my god, I could have walked." I gave him a stern look. "Hey, I made it out there on my own."

I couldn't stop myself from tasting those lips again, and his lips lifted in a smile I didn't need to see to feel in my bones. He buried his head in my neck as I stepped into the house from the cold and walked him over to the couch. "I'll be right back I'll go get your crutches."

"Wait." He gripped the front of my shirt as I tried to stand. "I don't need them, they can wait."

"What if you have to use the bathroom?"

"I wouldn't be opposed to you helping me." I lifted a brow and unclasped his hand before leaning in for one more taste. "Don't move. I'll help you to the bathroom when I get back." He grinned and pulled me back for a quick kiss before I hurried out of the room.

I put everything away and made sure nothing was plugged in or turned on before picking up the crutches and returning to Jordan. "Hey, sorry it took me so long, I was—"

He was still on the couch looking just as hot as he had when I'd left. There was just something about him that drew me to him. He was so chill and not at all arrogant or conceited. And he had every right to be. He pushed his hair back and it swept to the side, giving him an edgy look, but he didn't seem to play it up on purpose. Whatever it was I was digging it. At first, I thought he was a little nerdy, which is cute too. But the more time I spent with him and the longer we talked, I realized we were a lot alike. I expected him to be into computers and tech but he was more interested in working with his hands. Where woodworking was a hobby for me, being a mechanic was his profession and he seemed to enjoy it just as much.

"Do you need to use the bathroom? I should have asked before I went out to the shop."

"I was passed out by then, and I found it on my own. Not like there were many places it could be."

He grinned up at me from the couch and I walked straight to his side and sat down. "So, what do you want to do? Want to watch a movie? Or maybe play a game?"

"What games do you have?" He scooted up on the couch and adjusted his leg onto the coffee table.

"Name it, I have a lot of boardgames and card games: Yahtzee, Trivial Pursuit, Sorry, Uno, Life, Monopoly—"

"Monopoly, I haven't played it since I was a kid."

"Then Monopoly it is. Want to play the long game or the short version?" I took out the box from the closet and we both got busy setting it up on the table.

"The long game, we'll be here a few days, we got time." I smiled at that, glad to have his company on my time off. He had to adjust his leg a few times before he found a place that was comfortable but finally, we were ready to go.

"What piece do you want?" I asked, and secretly hoped he didn't take the dog.

"I want the shoe." I handed it to him and put the dog next to it on the Go space. A few hours later it hit me. This was one of the best nights I'd had since I'd moved here. And it just figured he'd be leaving after a few days.

Eleven

Sleeping with the Boot

I WASN'T SURE WHAT made me go out to find Trace, but I was glad I did. Seeing him working out there using his hands, and seeing the passion written all over his face, was completely worth the pain it caused me to hobble out there. I knew the next few hours were not going to be fun, but I didn't want him to know that.

"Do you need a pain pill?" he asked.

Apparently, I wasn't fooling him at all. "I think so, I probably shouldn't have tried to go so far on the crutches. I'm really not very good on them yet."

"You'll be fine. They take some getting used to though." He walked over to the kitchen and brought me back a pill and a glass of water. "Why don't we figure out where you'll be sleeping before you get too out of it."

"Where do you want me to sleep? I'm fine anywhere. Your place is so cozy." I sunk deeper into the couch. "I'm glad you brought me here." I reached for his hand and squeezed it.

"Let me show you my room. If you want to sleep there, I can help you upstairs. Otherwise, you get the couch."

"Your couch is very comfortable, but I want to see your room."

"Your wish—and all that."

Without any warning he scooped me up and carried me up the stairs like he did this every day and it wasn't a big deal. I burrowed in as close as I could to his chest. He smelled so good, I wasn't sure if it was his soap or just the way he smelled. But whatever it was, I wanted more of it.

"Well, what do you think?" The room was situated in the top of the A-frame house with a short railing overlooking the living room and kitchen. His bed almost filled the whole space with a large headboard and footboard made of heavy branches formed into a ladder rail.

"This is amazing. Your bed is beautiful."

"Thank you, I made it myself." He glanced at me with a look of pride. It was easy to see he enjoyed the compliment almost as much as he enjoyed the craft. "There's a small bathroom over there, I'll leave you here and bring up your things."

"Thanks, oh can I get a glass of water? I'm still thirsty for some reason."

"Probably the pain meds. I'll be right back."

I watched from the bed as he hurried down the stairs, grabbed two bottles of water and my suitcase, and walked back up.

"I love that you can see your whole place from up here."

"It's great, unless you have a visitor and you want privacy. There is no place in this house you can go where you can get away from another person."

"Good thing you don't have a roommate."

"That's how I know there's no privacy here. When I first moved here, I had a roommate that worked at another ski resort. We both tried, but it was a mutual decision that this place is meant for one person. Or maybe a couple. But definitely not two single guys."

I watched him as he moved around his room. Taking out pajamas from a drawer, pulling off his shirt and showing me a glimpse of his muscular chest with just a light smattering of dark hair. His eyes met mine and one side of his mouth tipped up in a grin when he realized I was staring.

"That damn dimple," I whispered, and held my hand out to him. He gifted me with a full-on smile before taking my hand and sitting next to me on the bed.

"I totally forgot; you were supposed to ice your leg. Let me get an ice pack and you can do it here."

"Sure, that sounds good. Do I need to take the boot off?"

"No, we'll work around it. I don't want you to cause yourself any pain. I'll unstrap the area we need to ice. Then the rest of it will be stable. Stay right here, and I'll go get it." He jumped up and was down the stairs before I could react, and in just a couple of minutes he was back.

"Let's get you ready for bed first."

I dug my pajamas out of my suitcase with his help. And realized I still had my ski clothes on. "I might need some help. I'm not sure how I'm supposed to get my pants off over this thing."

He smiled and knelt. "Try not to move it more than necessary. It's probably not going to feel good when I loosen the binding." He squeezed my knee and waited for me to answer.

"Go ahead, I can't sleep in these clothes, and at some point, I need to shower."

"Why don't we worry about that in the morning."

He unzipped the sides of my pants so there wasn't an issue pulling them off over the boot. I shimmied my ski pants and thermals down and he pulled them off my uninjured leg first, and carefully slid them down my broken leg, moving it just enough to pull them off. As he slid them off, he grabbed the pajama bottoms and slid those on. He was right it throbbed in a deep pain the whole time he was helping me, but I gritted my teeth and hoped he didn't notice how much pain I was in.

"Put your hands on my shoulders and I'll help you stand then I'll pull your pajamas the rest of the way up."

I pressed down on his shoulders and did all I could to keep the weight off my broken leg. He wasn't kidding that shit hurt. But not so much that I didn't see him pause for a moment to stare at my dick. I smirked and grimaced right after at the pain.

"Sorry." He pulled my pants up and sat me back on the bed. After strapping the boot back on, my leg continued to throb. "How's your pain level? It's still early for you to take another pain pill but if you need one you could take a half."

"Not great, but I want to spend a little time together before I pass out."

"If you're sure?" His eyes were so full of concern. Something that was new for me, and I found I really enjoyed it.

"I'm sure, but I do need to use the bathroom if you could help me?" He didn't hesitate to lift me into his arms again and carry me right to the bathroom.

"Do you need anything?"

"If you could bring me my shave kit, I'd appreciate it. It's right in the top of my suitcase." He walked away and was back in a flash. I held the door frame to balance, and as soon as he handed it to me, I kissed him thanks then closed the door. What a holiday this had turned out to be.

Twelve
Cold Nights and Warm Beds

I WALKED BACK TO the bedroom and changed into my pajamas. Seeing Jordan in his boxers was tempting enough. I didn't want to push it by undressing in front of him then having him get hurt if we got a little too crazy. I had to keep reminding myself he'd broken his leg not twenty-four hours ago.

Because I wanted to get a little crazy with him, god I wanted that so much. The connection I felt with him was so addictive. Every conversation and every kiss made me crave more time with him. Then like having a snowball land down the back of your jacket, I realized we only had a few days together. He'd be leaving soon, and I wasn't sure when we'd see each other again.

The door to the bathroom opened and I rushed over to help him back to the bedroom. "Hey, are you okay?"

"Yeah, I think I need to take it easy."

"Let me get you settled in."

"Sorry, I wanted to lie in bed and talk, or watch a movie or something other than sleep." His eyes looked weary even without another pill. I pulled the blankets back and helped him get covered up and tucked in. He shivered as he settled in, and I made sure he was on the side that his boot would be on the outside edge, so he didn't have to try to figure out where to rest it in the middle of the bed. I settled the icepack on his leg and hoped it wasn't going to get too cold.

"Are you comfortable?" He nodded, and his blinks got longer and slower.

"Your bed is so warm and comfy," he mumbled.

"It's warmer with you in it," I whispered as I slid into bed next to him and kissed his cheek. The corner of his mouth lifted in a grin and he pointed his finger to his lips. I laughed before complying. I wasn't a strong enough man to turn down a kiss to those lips.

He reached his hand out and gripped mine and pulled me close. "Snuggle with me."

I lay on my side and watched his steady breathing, and when he was asleep, I watched as he dreamed, and a smile ghosted across his lips. Fuck. Why couldn't I have met him when he wasn't leaving so soon?

"What's wrong?" Jordan turned to face me in the dark. I had no idea what had alerted him to the fact I was freaking out a little.

"Nothing, I thought you were asleep."

"You're a horrible liar. What is it?" He reached out his hand, cupped my jaw, and glided his thumb over my stubble.

"You'll think I'm crazy," I mumbled, and hoped he let it go.

"Now why would I do that? You've been amazing to me. We didn't know each other until this morning, and you didn't have to do anything for me at all. But you've shown me more kindness and care than a lot of people would. Way more than my friend did. He'll pay for that too just so you know." He grinned at me and cracked his eyes open.

"I feel such a strong connection to you. I'm not sure what it is. If it's the fact that you trusted me to take care of you, or that you're a mechanic and you work with your hands the way I do in my woodshop. Or maybe it's that spending time with you feels so familiar that I don't feel like I have to put on a show or do anything special to impress you. Not that you're easily impressed, I just mean—well, everything with you just feels so right."

His eyes opened wide at my words and for a moment I wasn't sure what his reaction would be. But he slipped his arm around me and pulled me to his chest. He kissed the top of my head, and I waited for his reply.

"I'm glad it was you that helped me. I know what you mean by it feeling so comfortable. It's hard for me to believe everything happened today. Let's just make the most of the time we have and not worry about when I'll leave. You might be so sick of me by then you can't wait."

"I doubt that." I put my arm across his stomach, and he wove his fingers with mine.

He finally fell asleep long before I did, as I imagined us doing a multitude of things together, and none of them included him being in a boot.

◆◆

I woke up a few hours later; it was cold in the house and I knew the fire had died down. I'd neglected to add a couple of logs before we'd gone to bed. Pulling my boots on I hoped there were enough coals left to light it without too much effort. The falling snow was visible through the windows at the front of the house.

Jordan was still sleeping, and had yet to move from the position he'd fallen asleep in. He wasn't kidding when he said pain meds knocked him out. I picked up the icepack that now lay on the floor, and hurried down the stairs trying to make as little noise as possible. I opened the door to the woodstove and sure enough it had all burned down. There was a good bed of coals, so I added a few logs and poked at it to get it going again. I held my hands out and enjoyed the heat before closing the door and standing there a minute longer.

"Trace?" Jordan called from my bed upstairs. I was so conflicted. I knew I should hold back and try to keep some distance. But I didn't want to waste the time we did have.

"Down here, I'm just putting more wood on the fire." He didn't answer and I thought he might have fallen back asleep, but then he peered over the railing.

"Come back to bed, I miss you."

The things this man did to my heart. Like I could say no to that.

Thirteen
Everything Good Ends

"You shouldn't be standing without your crutches," Trace said as he hurried up the stairs.

"I missed your warmth," I offered by way of explanation and hobbled toward the bed. Trace helped me along and pulled the blankets over me when I was settled again. He climbed in next to me and shuffled his feet under the blankets to warm them up.

"I missed your warmth too," he whispered and kissed me lightly. And like we did this every night and had a million more nights ahead of us, I fell asleep.

♦♦

Morning came far too soon, and this time when I woke up, the first thing I noticed was I was alone again. The second thing I noticed was how fucking sore I was, and when I moved the boot by mistake, how much my fucking leg hurt. "Ngah," I gritted out, and tried not to move or make any noise. Trace didn't need to know I was willing my leg to fall off so it would hopefully hurt less.

Footsteps running up the stairs told me he'd heard. "Jordan? Are you okay?"

His cool hands on my face gave me something else to focus on besides the throbbing pain in my leg and the multiple sore muscles that were all making their presence known loud and clear.

"Let me get you something to eat so you can take a pain pill. Then how does a shower sound?"

"Like heaven. But I'm not sure I can handle the boot while I'm in there."

"Don't worry. I've got a plan." He rummaged around and pulled out what looked like a pool toy, but when he inflated it, I realized it was an inflatable cast. "What do you think?"

"I think I can't wait to take a shower."

He deflated it and helped me down the stairs to the kitchen. "Stay right there, and I'll make you some toast and eggs. How does that sound?"

"Sounds good to me. Got any coffee?"

He responded with a "pssh" and as if on cue, a coffee maker on the counter started to drip.

"I have it scheduled. I need my caffeine every morning."

"Smart man, I kinda love you right now." I froze for a second and hoped he didn't hear me, but he turned the full power of his dimple on me and I knew for a fact he'd heard every word. "Sorry, I think I need that coffee more than I realized."

"Oh, I don't mind at all. In fact, it's kinda nice to have someone appreciate me."

I knew he was joking, but I did appreciate him. I could have been sitting by myself in my hotel room doing nothing, waiting for Dave to come back and hopefully bring me something to eat. This was so much better.

"Are you sure you don't mind me taking up your time? You can take me back to the hotel if you have plans or if you just want some privacy."

He turned from the toaster where he was putting a couple of slices of bread, and walked over to where I sat on the other side of the bar. Taking my face in his hands, he kissed me. It was slow, and warm, and soft, tasting of toothpaste and a hint of coffee. And it was so fucking perfect I knew for a fact I would never forget it, and I'd spend the rest of my life trying to duplicate it. My eyes fluttered open to find him still so close I wanted to have one more taste. His returning grin told me he suspected what I was thinking.

"Don't move. I'm going to give you some toast so you can take a pain pill. Are you still hurting?"

"I wasn't a minute ago but now I am." The pain came roaring back reminding me I had a broken bone and that I'd probably crashed way harder than I thought I had. He didn't wait, just buttered the toast that had popped up and slid it to me along with the bottle of pain pills. "Thanks." I nibbled the toast and swallowed down the pill with a glass of water he'd given to me.

I watched as he moved around the kitchen just as confident as he was when he was helping me off the mountain. While he cooked, we shared glances that I'd miss once I was home. Fuck. I didn't want to think about that. I'd just enjoy the time I had here, even if it was flying by way too fast.

"When do you go back?" Trace asked without looking up from the eggs he was now cooking.

"Tomorrow. We have an early flight because we both work on Monday. Which reminds me, I need to call my boss and let him know I'll have to figure out a way to work."

"You could try one of those scooters. They're a lot easier than crutches, and you should be able to work on it. I mean, unless you have to crawl under a car, but I'll let you figure out how to do that."

He grinned at me, and I knew I was going to miss that smile more than I was willing to think about. "I hadn't thought of that, good idea. I'll check and see where I can find one in Sacramento."

"If you want, we can check out Salt Lake City. You could pick it up on the way to the airport. It would make your life much easier when you're waiting for your flight."

"I'll get my laptop out and see what I can find. And I probably need to charge my phone. I was so out of it last night I didn't remember to put it on the charger."

"I plugged it in while you were in the bathroom. I thought you might need it."

"Thank you, Trace." God every minute was making it harder to leave. He handed me my phone and I pretended to check messages while trying to figure out how I'd leave and not tear my heart in half.

Fourteen
Fun and Games and Emotion

"Did you hear from your friend?" Trace asked, as he cleaned up after breakfast.

"Yeah, he's skiing again today. Said he's having the best time he's ever had. The dick." I laughed at my words. Dave was a dick, but he was also there for me many times when no one else was.

"If you're ready I can help you in the shower."

"Oh, a man after my heart. That would make my day."

Without another word he scooped me up and carried me up the stairs.

"You're spoiling me, I'm going to expect to be carried from now on."

He planted a loud kiss on my lips and smiled. "I can handle that."

"I bet you can," I murmured as he sat me on the foot of the bed. "So, how are we doing this?"

"I'm going to remove off your boot and you can slip off your clothes. Let me get you a robe." He darted into the bathroom and came back with a fluffy white robe. "Take off your shirt and slip it on."

I did as he instructed, and he knelt in front of me and started to loosen the boot. As soon as the pressure was released and the accompanying stability was gone, my leg screamed. I clenched my teeth and tried not to focus on it but there was no way in hell. It hurt, and I couldn't fake it.

"Hurry and slip out of your pants and I'll put the temporary boot on. It'll help. Once you're all cleaned up you can go without a shower until you get home."

I nodded and slipped my pajamas and boxers down all at once not giving a shit what he saw. All I cared about was making the pain end. Pulling the robe tighter around me, I closed my eyes and hoped it didn't take long to put the other boot on. As he inflated it, the pain started to subside, but it didn't go away.

"Don't worry, there's a seat in the shower. I'm going to turn on the water so it's warm. Try to relax until I get back."

I heard him step away, and I focused on slowing my breathing and trying to get the pain under control. The water came on and in just a few seconds he was back. "I'm sorry, I know it's painful. But you'll feel so much better after a shower. Trust me." He nuzzled into my neck, and I worried what I smelled like but then I focused on how good he felt, and how safe *I* felt when he was close.

"Let's do this. I know it'll be worth it." He didn't hesitate; just lifted me and carried me into the bathroom. It was big enough for both of us to walk into no problem. After he made sure I was settled on the counter next to the sink, he reached to check the temperature of the water.

Without another a word, he turned around and stripped out of his pajamas before I had a chance to realize what he was doing. Without a word he slipped the robe off my shoulders and carried me into the shower keeping his back to the spray until he had me settled on the seat at the far end.

Finally, I took a chance and glanced at his body. He was long and lean, his back muscles flexed as he squeezed some shower gel between his hands and worked it into a lather. He turned and without wasting another moment he soaped up my leg above the cast and moved to my other leg. He took the shower attachment off and used it to wet my hair after he rinsed off my legs. "That feels so good," I groaned.

"You're going to love this then." He washed my hair, and I had to admit I did love it. His fingers dug in and scrubbed my scalp and massaged my neck. "Hold your hand out."

He squirted some bodywash in my hand and I soaped up my chest and arms while he did a quick wash on himself with his back turned and his face in the water. When he turned around to face me again, he leaned over and kissed me; it was warm and wet, and it was one more kiss I never wanted to forget.

"What is it with you?" he whispered as he rested his forehead against mine.

My eyes slid shut and I concentrated on every place I felt his touch. His breath was warm against my face and he reached up and stroked my cheek with his thumb. My hand covered his and I soaked him in hoping this moment lasted just a little longer. His hands slid down my back and he pulled me closer to him as he leaned in as close as he could. "We should probably get out. I don't want your leg to start hurting."

"It already hurts, but I don't care." He pulled back and met my eyes, before I pulled him back to me. "This is worth it. You're worth it."

He held me a moment more before he kissed me and stood. Seeing him on full display was something I wouldn't ever get enough of. The reappearance of that damn dimple, and his knowing smirk, let me know he was well aware of where my mind had gone. He turned the water off and grabbed a towel and wrapped me up in it before he dried himself. I did the best I could from a seated position, and after he tucked his towel around his waist, he picked me up again and carried me back to the bedroom.

"Don't move, I'll get you something to wear." He rummaged around in his drawers and brought back some flannel pants and a t-shirt. I slipped the shirt on and after he pulled the pants over the temporary cast, I pulled them all the way up. "I'm going to try to do this as fast as I can. When I deflate it, I'm not sure how it's going to feel. But I'll get the boot back on quick."

I nodded and braced for the pain I knew would follow, but he changed it out so fast that the discomfort was minimal. Or maybe the pain meds had really kicked in. The heaviness in my eyes told me the latter was true.

"Let's get you ready for a nap," he whispered as I fell fast asleep in his warm, comfortable bed.

Fifteen
One Last Night

Like a creepy stalker, I sat on the other side of the bed and watched Jordan as he slept. He was hot, there was no denying that, but what was so special about him that pulled me in and left me no choice but to go to him? Even now, knowing he'd be leaving tomorrow morning, I couldn't stand to be apart from him even if he was asleep.

I lowered myself down next to him and took his hand in mine. He tried to turn and snuggle into me, but his boot held him back, so I slid closer and curled up into his side. I'd miss this so much. It had been so long since I'd had anyone to spend a quiet afternoon with and I wanted to cherish it. Tomorrow after he'd left, my life would go back to how it had been. Work, cooking, woodworking, and anything else that kept me busy. I drifted off to sleep imagining us doing far more than what we were able to do now and dreamed of us having as much time as we wanted together. And I think that was when I realized how hard it would be to say good-bye.

◆◆

A short time later, I awoke to Jordan propped up on his elbow staring at me.

"Hello," he said with a smile.

"Hey," I answered, and dragged the tips of my fingers against the side of his head.

"It must be time to wake up and eat again," he laughed as the words left his mouth.

"Must be. What time did you say your flight leaves?"

"Sunday morning at seven."

"Tomorrow will be an early morning then."

He sat up and blinked. "Is it tomorrow? I think I lost a day somewhere. I thought I still had another day here." He rubbed his eyes and looked a little more awake after.

"Well, we'll just have to make the most of what's left of today. Let me cook you a nice dinner and we can watch a movie or play a game. Whatever you want."

"That sounds great, I'm glad I get to spend another night with you."

His phone beeped, and he reached across to where I'd set it on the side table.

"Dave. He's just checking to make sure I'll be ready to go."

"Are you?" I tried not to ask, but we were out of time, and I didn't want to regret keeping my thoughts to myself later.

"Honestly? No, I'd rather stay here. These past couple of days have been amazing. I mean besides the broken leg—that part sucked. But spending time with you in your cozy house has me wanting more time here. I'm really going to miss you," he whispered the last part, and I pulled him back to me.

"Come on, let's go downstairs and make the most of today. How's your pain?"

"It's there, but I don't want to take more pills. I want to stay awake the rest of the day."

I looked him in the eyes, and he didn't seem to be in any pain. "If it gets bad you could try some ibuprofen. But let me know if it's too much."

"I will. Now let's go downstairs and pick a movie to watch."

I carried him down and settled him on the couch with the remote. "Pick something, I'm going to start dinner. I want to cook something special."

There was a recipe I wanted to try, I'd never cooked it before, but I knew I had most of the ingredients. What better reason to finally try Beef Wellington—well mini ones. Most of the ingredients were in the freezer so I gathered what I needed and set about thawing them. It was still early afternoon so there was enough time. The microwave slowly thawed the steaks while I made sure I had everything else.

"Did you pick a movie?" I said across the counter.

"I picked a few, we can decide together."

"Give me just a minute and I'll be ready to go." This all felt so natural, and so domestic. I stopped my prep work and watched as Jordan flipped through the menu. Stopping at some titles and scrolling past others. I knew so little about him. I had no clue what movies he liked or what he couldn't stand. But damn I wished I had the time to find out.

"Sounds good. There's so much to choose from, the more I look the more I find."

"Did you need to go back to your hotel before tomorrow?"

"No, Dave's taking care of it. Thanks to you, I have all my things and the room was in his name. It's the least he can do." He looked back and grinned at me making me grin back. I took the tenderloin steaks out and seasoned them while I waited for the mushrooms to sauté. Once I had all the ingredients ready, I placed the beef and mushrooms in the puff pastry dough and made sure I'd added everything else.

I then put together a quick green salad and wiped my hands off before joining Jordan on the couch while it cooked.

"So, what did you pick?" I asked as I settled in next to him.

"I found a few Christmas movies. I didn't get a chance to watch many this year. Do you mind?"

"Are you kidding? I love it, what are we watching first?"

"Love Actually? It's sort of a tradition for me. I try to watch it every year."

"I haven't watched that for a while. It sounds perfect." He settled back against me with his boot on the couch, and we watched as the characters bumbled their way through their Christmas romances. When the timer went off, I jumped up and took the Wellingtons out of the oven.

"I don't know what you've cooked but whatever it is, it smells amazing."

"Thank you, Jordan, now hopefully it tastes just as good." I warmed up a loaf of sourdough and put everything on a wooden tray to take into the living room. After setting it on the coffee table, I lit a few candles, and poured us both some sparkling cider. Jordan hadn't taken a pain med yet, but I didn't want to take the chance of him needing one and having a bad reaction after a glass of wine.

"Trace, this looks and smells amazing. I wish I got to come home to this every night."

My eyes shot to his, but he was focused on the tray of food. Somewhere deep inside I wished for the same thing but barring a severe storm that made it impossible to get to Salt Lake City, I didn't see that happening.

"Thanks, let's dig in." I pushed those thoughts and feelings down once again and focused on what we had right now. Even if I knew it wouldn't ever be enough.

Sixteen
Gone But Not Forgotten

WE WATCHED THE END of Love Actually, and after eating the amazing dinner Trace had cooked, I was starting to get sleepy. He suggested a nap so after encouraging me to put my head in his lap, I fell right to sleep. I wanted to enjoy all the time we had left, but I was so tired.

The sound of the television woke me a while later, and I realized Trace was no longer there. I pushed myself up and squeezed my eyes shut and blinked them open again, trying to wake up. "Trace?"

"Over here," he said from the back of the house. He walked into the living room carrying a few pieces of wood. "Sorry, it was starting to get cold in here." He added a few logs to the woodstove and moved back to my side. "Want to watch another movie?"

"No, I think I'm ready for bed. I need to get up really early. Dave said he'll be here around four in the morning."

"Let's get you ready then." He smiled at me, and it somehow didn't look right. Which was probably exactly how my smile looked too. So much of this was wrong, and I was having a really hard time processing it all. My thoughts were interrupted by Trace lifting me off the couch and holding me close. He rested his forehead against mine for a moment before inhaling and walking up the stairs.

"You really amaze me. Not many guys could carry me around like you have."

"It's part of my training. I need to be able to move an injured person. Plus moving you around has not been a hardship."

"I really appreciate all you've done," I told him as he settled me on the bed. "Can I ask you something?"

His face softened and he brushed his thumb along my jaw. "You can ask me anything. What is it?"

"Well, outside it looks like Christmas exploded all over your house, but there are no decorations inside. Not even a tree. Why is that?" He propped a pillow under my head and scooted closer to my side.

"I love Christmas, the lights, the decorations, literally everything about it. But I don't have any family here, and I rarely have anyone over. I used to decorate but then it seemed to make more sense to decorate outside rather than inside. People would drive by and comment on all the decorations, so it felt like I was sharing it with everyone, and not just hiding it all away for myself. Does that make sense?"

I reached my hand out for his and squeezed it when our fingers wove together like they knew exactly how we fit. "It makes sense. If I lived here, I'd spend every Christmas with you so we could decorate the whole place. You could make all sorts of wooden Christmas decorations and we could string lights all over the place. You could cook us a great meal from one of the millions of recipes I know you're dying to try. We'd be happy. Just you and me. That's all we'd need." His eyes met mine and he smiled and leaned forward to kiss me.

"I'd like that. Maybe someday you'll come back and visit me." His voice held so much longing, so much raw emotion, holding hands with him wasn't enough. I pulled him close and lay his head on my chest. I stroked his hair as we both drifted off, and the whole time I hoped this wasn't all we had.

My phone woke me a while later. It was still dark out, and through the window I could see the snow slowly drifting down in the lights from the outside of the house. It was beautiful. Just like everything with Trace.

"I'm awake," he mumbled, but I wasn't sure he really was.

"It's okay, Dave will be here soon. I just need to change my clothes and brush my teeth. Hopefully I can get one of those scooters on the way to the airport."

"Wait, I can take you. I was planning on going." He sat up looking sleep rumpled and gorgeous in the clothes he'd worn last night. He cleared his throat and rubbed his eyes as I lifted the boot and set it down on the floor beside the bed. "Don't try to stand on it. I'll help you."

"Thank you, Trace. What will I do without my hero?" He scooped me up and held me close for a moment before taking me into the bathroom. It had only been a couple of days, but we had a pretty good routine now. And hopefully once I had a cast on and could put some weight on my leg, I'd be able to take care of myself. Trace settled me on the sink while I dug out my toothbrush and deodorant. I'd shave later—that didn't matter now.

"I'll leave you while I go change. Do you want your suitcase?"

"I just need a change of clothes." He walked out and quickly returned with a pair of my pants and a shirt.

"When you're ready to put the pants on let me know and I'll help you with the boot." I nodded and slid off the counter to my good foot. He closed the door and I got busy doing everything I needed to do.

It was still dark out, and I hated that I wouldn't get to see more of his place in the daylight. Trace had helped me back to his bedroom and together we worked out how to put the boot over my pants. I was thankful it wasn't a long flight home, but I was nervous about having to pull my suitcase while trying to navigate the airport. My phone buzzed with a message, and I reached again for my phone.

"It's Dave, he says he'll be here in fifteen minutes."

"Oh, I didn't realize he'd be here so soon," Trace said, and looked everywhere he could except at me.

"Give me your number, I want to make sure we can stay in touch. And, Trace, I promise this isn't the end. I promise." His eyes met mine, and he smiled. And if I hadn't spent the past couple of days with him, I'd think he really was happy. But that wasn't a happy smile, I was sure of that. I tapped out a text to the number he gave me and when he sent a text back, I saved his information to my contacts.

We were just getting to the bottom of the stairs when a car horn honked out front. Our eyes locked as he carried me down to the couch.

"I put your suitcase by the door. If you're ready to go I'll help you out to the car."

"That would be great, thanks, Trace."

He scooped me up and kissed me goodbye from where he stood outside the car with the door open. "I'll call as soon as I get back to Sacramento."

"Okay and, Jordan?"

"Yeah, Trace?"

"I won't forget, and I want this as bad as you do. This isn't the end, it's the beginning." His voice cracked a little with emotion, and I knew those words did not come easy for him. He was a strong man, and this was hurting him as much as it was me.

"Sorry, guys, but we really gotta get going if we're going to rent you a scooter and get to the flight on time," Dave said from the driver's seat. I didn't waste another second and pulled Trace in for one more kiss, and whispered promises to talk later. It was so much harder to drive away than I would have ever expected. As we pulled away from the warm house with all the lights and Christmas decorations on it, I worried I'd never see it, or him, again.

Seventeen
Not That Ending

AS SOON AS THEIR car was out of sight, my heart pulled me in a direction I never would have anticipated. I stood there, my feet planted until the glow of taillights was long gone, but still, I didn't move. The feel of his warm lips on mine, and the taste of him still lingered , but it wasn't enough. I traced my fingers along my lips, as I stood outside in the cold in the early morning of a new day. A new day that would begin with me all alone. Something I used to crave after all the craziness of my job, but now . . . it only felt lonely.

I squeezed my eyes shut and clenched my teeth to control the shivers that threatened to overwhelm my senses.

My arms squeezed my middle so tight my hands shook with the effort. Throwing my head back I looked up at the sky above me as a few feathery flakes fell, and I tried like hell not to think of Jordan, but he held my every thought. Finally, I forced myself to walk back into the house, the warmth of the cabin making my skin hurt where the cold had penetrated.

What the hell was wrong with me? I hardly knew this guy. I'd only spent a couple of days with him, but when he left it was like I was being torn apart. I sat on the couch and noticed a notebook I'd seen Jordan writing in occasionally. I picked it up and flipped it open expecting to see a list of things he didn't want to forget before he left. But instead, there was only a few words written.

Ask Trace for his number, and don't leave until you get it. Don't blow it.

I huffed out a laugh when I read it not really sure why he'd feel the need to write it down but feeling a little giddy that he had. I flipped through the other pages and didn't see anything else until I looked on the back of the last page.

Love?

He really did feel it too! I was in motion before my mind caught up with my body. I jogged upstairs and pulled some jeans on with a warm shirt and rushed through brushing my teeth. There was only one way to know for sure, and as stupid an idea as it was, and highly unlikely that it would work, I grabbed my phone and ran for my truck.

"What are you doing?" I said into the cold early morning air as I flung open the door and dove in. I tore out of there like I would if I was headed for an emergency, and I was. The only difference was this was an emergency of the heart—my heart that would never let me forgive myself for letting him go without a fight.

It had snowed lightly through the night, nothing that I couldn't handle. And, I hoped it snowed enough to slow them down in their car. As I left the city limits of Park City, I once again questioned my sanity, but again I knew I couldn't live with myself if I didn't try.

♦♦

The snow slowed me down a little, but I still made it to the airport in less than an hour, and after driving around the parking lot I was lucky enough to find a parking space fairly close and bolted for the terminal. Jordan had mentioned they were flying out on Southwest, so I didn't waste any time and ran right for it. I burst through the front doors into a wall of people. Everyone was standing around with their luggage at their feet, waiting to check-in. All the counters at Southwest looked the same, then I heard an announcement over the PA system.

"Ladies and gentlemen, we at Southwest would like to apologize for the longer than normal wait times. Our computer system has gone down, so as soon as we're up and running again we'll be able to get you all checked-in and on your way. Until then we'll be manually checking you in. Your patience is appreciated. Thank you."

I ignored the loud groan from the passengers, as I rushed to each line and checked every person, but there were so many people and so much luggage, it all blended into one big mass of humanity. I was ready to give up when suddenly I spotted him. He was sitting on his suitcase with his leg propped out in front of him. His crutches were under his arms, and his head was bowed. I walked straight up to him and knelt by his extended leg and reached out my hand to push through his hair.

His sleepy eyes looked up, and when he realized it was me, he lunged and nearly knocked me off my feet. I laughed and caught him before we both tumbled over and stood holding him to me.

"Trace? What are you doing here?"

"I couldn't let you leave. It's not time yet. Stay with me, at least until your leg heals. I didn't realize how much I loved having you there until you weren't. It's not the same without you, Jordan. Stay, just a while longer." I held him at arm's-length and his eyes locked with mine.

"I'll stay as long as you'll let me."

"You mean it?" I asked. Wanting to believe it with all my heart, but afraid he didn't really mean it.

"I mean it." He leaned forward to kiss me.

"Jordan, what the fuck are you talking about. You're supposed to work tomorrow," Dave said from behind Jordan.

"Broken leg, remember that part? I won't be working for a while. I can't put any weight on it until I get it in a cast like I've told you a few times."

"Did you get a scooter?" I asked and looked between the two of them. Jordan shot Dave a look and Dave cringed and stepped back.

"Jordan told me where you told him to go, but I thought we could rent one here. I was wrong."

"Have you been trying to use your crutches and pull your suitcase?" My voice rose at the knowledge. He couldn't handle the crutches around the house, there was no way in hell he could handle them at the airport in the best of conditions. He didn't have to answer for me to know. "Okay, let's go." I scooped him up and Dave rushed to hand him his crutches.

"I'll need to go get my truck. Dave, how about you bring Jordan's suitcase and crutches out front for him?"

"But I'll lose my—of course." He asked the person behind him to save his place, and since the line still wasn't moving, I knew he'd be fine. We all stepped out into the brisk morning air, and I found a bench for Jordan to sit.

"I'll be right back. I parked close." I turned to walk away but spun around and took his face in my hands. I kissed him with a loud smack before rushing off to get my truck.

This was right, him and me, and whatever we had between us. And I couldn't wait to get him home and explore all those feelings.

Eighteen
The Beginning of Us

"Are you sure this is what you want?" Dave asked, concern written all over his face as he held my crutches.

"Here give me those. Yes, I'm sure. Don't worry; I sent a text to Lonny and told him what happened. He knows I can't work until I get a cast and that's going to be at least a week. I might as well spend it here."

"Okay, if you're sure."

"I am. Trace is a good guy. He's really helped me out."

"I'm sorry all this happened. I should have been more careful and made sure you were behind me."

"Dave, if this hadn't happened there's no way, I would have met him. So really, I owe you one." I smiled at that, knowing it would ease some of his guilt, and realizing everything I said was true.

"Okay, if you're sure. I'm going to go back before the line moves. Call me later okay?"

"You got it, thanks again, Dave." He waved as he walked back into the terminal and I turned toward the direction Trace had gone. There was no way I could hold back my smile when I recognized his truck, and his answering smile told me I was making the right choice.

"I got it," he said, when he hurried over to me and picked up the crutches and my suitcase and put them behind the seat. When he walked back to me he didn't hesitate to pick me back up.

"I think you enjoy this." I grinned at him and rested my head against his chest.

"I know I enjoy this." He kissed the top of my head before easing me into the truck, and after clicking me into the seatbelt and another quick kiss, he ran around to the driver's side. He reached across the seat and squeezed my hand as he pulled away from the curb.

"How does some breakfast sound before we go find you a scooter?"

"Sounds like a plan. Then I'll probably need a nap."

"You can have whatever you want." His eyes were so bright and full of emotions I didn't want to name for fear I was wrong. But hopefully soon, I'd know for sure.

◆◆

After a big breakfast, and a little extra caffeine, we were on our way to find a scooter.

"I still can't believe Dave thought you'd be fine at the airport. He and I will be talking about his choices at some point."

"I think you scared him." I laughed and squeezed Trace's hand. "He's really not that bad, but he is clueless. I can't imagine him doing something to hurt me on purpose, he's just not a very good planner."

"We'll see. But he needs to know now that I'm around he won't be getting away with that crap." I smiled at that, he had no clue how truly forgetful Dave was, but I guess if he was around me long enough, eventually he'd find out.

We pulled up to a Walmart he said would have a scooter. "Did you want to try your crutches?"

"Sure, I've got to get used to them at some point." I was unsteady, and couldn't seem to get it down very well, but I made it into the store under my own power and was relieved when he directed me to a ride-on cart. "This is so much easier." I grinned and glided along at zero point two miles per hour. "I could hop this up a little, give it a little more horsepower."

"You'll be faster on the scooter." Trace smiled down at me. We found the scooter easy enough and faster than I would have thought possible, we were in his truck headed for his house. "You're sure about me staying? I know you have responsibilities there. If you want to go, I'll go with you. I don't want you to regret staying."

I turned to look at him, the early morning and throbbing in my leg getting the better of me. My eyes tried to close, but I fought them, wanting to enjoy how he looked when he wasn't able to look back at me, but I was too tired and fell asleep before we'd left the city limits of Salt Lake City.

♦♦

Home. After a short drive, and a nap that wasn't nearly long enough, we pulled up to Trace's house. I'm not sure why, but it felt like home to me more than my own house did. Probably because he made it feel so warm and welcoming with all the personal touches, he probably didn't even realize made me feel so comfortable here. He lifted me out of the seat and carried me into the house to the sofa. Before he could slip away, I reached for his hand. "Trace, thank you for coming after me. I've never had anyone do something like that. It was pretty amazing, and I think Dave will always be looking behind him when you're around."

He laughed and sat down on the couch next to me. "I'll be just a minute, I need to bring everything in. But I'm so damn glad you came back. This house feels so much more alive with you in it. I like it."

"I like it too, now go get my crap and let's take a nap."

"Such a sweet talker," he mumbled before kissing me.

I watched as he walked out the door not knowing what our future held or if there was a future there at all. But secure in the knowledge that both of us were willing to explore exactly what we had between us.

"So, what do you usually do for New Year's Eve?" he asked as he kicked the door shut behind him and set down the suitcase and crutches. "I'll go back for the scooter in a minute."

"Come here and sit, we've got time. Now to answer your question, I usually don't do much of anything for New Year's Eve, but I think I'd love to spend that night here with you."

"Yeah?" he whispered his voice gravely smooth.

"Yeah. Maybe by then I'll have a cast and you won't have to carry me all over the place."

"Oh, I don't mind that, not at all."

"Good thing, because I think your bed is calling my name, care to join me?"

"Anytime, and anywhere." He scooped me up and carried me upstairs, and after a pain pill, as we lay in bed warm and snug, and hidden away from the world once again, I couldn't think of anywhere else I'd rather be.

Nineteen
A Short Ride

"Jordan, I called the medical center, and Lissa was able to get you in later this afternoon to get your leg checked out and hopefully a cast put on." We'd spent a quiet evening last night barely leaving the bedroom. It was warm and cozy and everything we both needed.

"What about your ex?" he asked with a smirk.

"Eh, if he's there I can ignore him. I don't mind calling another office if you'd rather . . ."

"Nope, I'm fine with seeing Dr. Dreamy."

I met his eyes and he held my gaze for a full second before he burst out laughing.

"Oh my god your face. I'm sorry, Trace, he really is a dick." I pulled him in for a hug, mindful of his boot, and kissing him on the head.

"Yep, he is. Now why don't we go see what's for breakfast?" I scooped him up, carried him to the bar, and set him down so I could get busy. "What sounds good?"

"Surprise me, you know I love everything you've cooked so far."

I decided on French toast and got busy cracking eggs and slicing bread from a loaf I'd made a few days ago. I put it all together and fried up some bacon because who didn't like bacon. Jordan was silent as I moved around the kitchen, but every time I looked in his direction, I found him looking back at me with a smile on his face.

"You really enjoy cooking," he said, more like he was confirming it rather than questioning.

"I do, it quiets my mind. When things are stressful, or I'm being pulled too many directions and feel like I'll explode, cooking always calms me. I'm not sure why." I drained the bacon and plated the French toast.

"I feel that way when I'm working on a car. I know it's not for everyone, and some people look down on us, but I love it."

"They better not look down on you if they want their car fixed," I said as I passed him a plate.

"Yeah, funny how that works. They might talk down to us when we're out and about, but when they bring their car in, they're sweet as can be." He took a bite of his French toast after spreading butter and syrup all over it.

"That noise should be illegal," I said, my own fork held just in front of my mouth.

"I'm sure I don't know what you mean," he said without looking up from his plate and continuing to eat. I couldn't tear my eyes away from him for a second, as he continued to ignore me and focus on his breakfast. Just as I was about to look down, his eyes met mine, twinkling with a glint of humor.

"Sure you don't." The heat in the room seemed to rise as we leaned against each other and finished eating.

My phone dinged with a message interrupting what we were about to start. "Lissa sent a text; they're really slow right now, so it's a perfect time to go if you're ready."

"I am so ready! I should probably change though."

He had on sweatpants and a t-shirt which looked fine to me. I shrugged my shoulder at him. "I think it's fine. You'll want to wear something loose enough to fit over a cast. Those pants are perfect; throw on your coat and you're good to go."

He glided on his scooter toward the door and slipped on his coat before he turned to me and smiled, and without another word I scooped him up and carried him out to the truck.

"What are you doing?" he laughed. "I need my scooter."

"I know." I kissed him as I set him in the front seat. "I'll get it." After making sure he was settled I jogged to the front door and brought back his scooter.

"Thanks, babe," he said, as I slid into the driver's seat.

"Babe? I could get used to that."

"Yeah?" he breathed out and leaned back on the headrest.

"Yeah." I leaned in and kissed those lips I couldn't resist for one more second. My lips moved across his, and warmth spread through me that had nothing to do with the heater in the truck. I pressed my forehead against his as we both caught our breath. "You sure you need that cast?" I whispered, before huffing out a soft laugh.

"I was sure, but right now not so much."

I squeezed his shoulder and turned back to face the steering wheel. "Come on, let's get this done then we can see what other trouble we can get into."

"Oh, I like the sound of that. Babe."

I glanced at him in time to see his smirk as we pulled away from my house. The streets were quiet, the snow keeping the shoppers and tourists in their cabins and hotels. That would change later on when the restaurants and bars would be open to welcome them with warm food and conversation.

"So, you really like living here?" he asked.

"Yeah, it's constantly changing and there's always something new to see. Even with the tourists it's a great place to live. I mean, besides the snow."

"It's beautiful here. The downtown area reminds me a little of Old Town Sacramento."

"I've never been there. What's it like?"

"Busy, the freeway traffic sucks. But once you get into the neighborhoods it's a great place to live. Lots of places to go out and eat, close to Tahoe and the beach. It's a perfect location."

"Sounds like it. We're not close to anything out here. Well except more ski areas and Salt Lake City."

"Well that's not so bad. There's a lot going on in town; if I lived here, I wouldn't ever want to leave."

"Really?" I was curious how he felt about Park City. I knew it wasn't for everyone. The turnover we had at the ski area was proof of that. A lot of people came here for one season and were long gone by the next.

"Yeah, I saw they have a mountain bike track at Park City ski area. I'd like to try it in the summer."

"You mountain bike?" There was so much I didn't know about Jordan. And so much I wanted to know.

"Yep, I live close enough to the American River Bike Trail I ride it as often as I can. But I really enjoy going out on some of the other trails."

"We'll have to go sometime," I offered.

"I'd like that." He took my hand as we pulled into the parking lot for the medical center.

I parked the truck and turned to face him. "There's so much more I want to know about you."

"The feeling is mutual. Now, get me in there so I can get this leg taken care of so that we can hopefully do more than just watch TV together."

"Hey, we've cooked and played games."

"You cooked, and I am more than happy to watch you do that anytime."

A knock on the window startled us both. As I clenched my fist near my heart, my eyes shot to the window to see Drake with his hand raised to knock again, and a shit-eating grin on his face. *Asshole.*

"You guys going in or you gonna sit out here all day?" he asked before turning to jog back to the building.

"God he's such an—" Jordan started.

"Asshole," I finished, and slid out of the truck.

"He really is," Jordan mumbled into my chest, as I carried him to the door.

Twenty
Finally, A Cast

TRACE CARRIED ME INTO the medical center and rushed back out to get my scooter. As soon as he was out the door his ex was back.

"Hey there, you ready to get a cast?"

"So ready." I tried to pretend he wasn't as annoying as he was, but then I realized he probably didn't care either way.

Trace walked back in with my scooter and set it on the ground near me. As soon as I was mobile again, Doctor Flynn led me back to a room where the nurse, Lissa, was setting up a few items on a tray.

"Have a seat on the exam table. This won't take too long," Lissa said.

I climbed up and sat back so my leg was on the table. The doctor immediately unstrapped the boot and examined my leg.

"Not much swelling, it looks good. Once you have the cast you'll be able to move around a bit more. It's not as heavy as the boot, but you still won't be able to bear weight on it for a while. We'll give it a few weeks then put you in a walking cast or another boot. Until then you're stuck with the scooter."

"That's okay. I expected it."

"Good thing you have Trace here to keep you company."

"Yeah, I'm lucky to have someone like him around." Trace's eyes locked on mine, and I didn't give a fuck if his ex knew there was more between us than him just being a nice guy and helping me out.

"Okay then," the doctor said, and got busy putting the cast on. "Any color preference?"

"Nope, not at all."

"How about red?" Trace said from next to me.

"Red it is," the doctor said, not taking the time to look up from whatever he was doing.

Trace reached for my hand and held it as my leg was wrapped and finally a cast was fitted. "There's no way I could have worked with this," I mumbled.

"What do you do for a living?" Lissa asked.

"Mechanic back in Sacramento, California."

"I don't think you'll be doing that for a while. Maybe simple things, but the first few weeks you'll have to watch out for swelling if you're standing too long."

"I'll make sure he does what he's supposed to do," Trace said, and squeezed my hand. The doctor looked between the two of us and rolled his eyes.

"Thanks, Trace." I smiled at him, and he squeezed my hand again.

"How's your pain been?"

"Not bad, I haven't needed a pain med yet today."

"You will when we're done. I guess Trace has done a pretty good job of taking care of you," Doctor Flynn said, without looking at either of us. It may have been the one time in his life he admitted someone was doing a good job without bragging about how much better he could do it. I didn't know him at all, but I knew his type.

I looked up at Trace to find him looking at me, not even giving his ex any attention at all.

"So how much longer are you staying? I mean, you can't just stay here indefinitely can you?" the doctor asked, and I wondered why it was any of his business.

"Well, I haven't thought about that yet. But—"

"I have this week off, he can decide for himself when he's ready to go back home. Not that it's any of your business." Trace gave him a look that would have made me flinch, but Doctor Flynn just ignored it and kept working.

"Okay you're good to go. Take it easy the next few hours. It's set but it won't hurt to let the cast cure just a little longer, and if you do end up leaving at the end of the week then good luck." With that he walked out of the room and left Lissa to clean up the mess.

"Sorry, Trace, he was supposed to go to lunch. You must have caught him just as he was leaving," she whispered, and clenched her teeth with an *oops* look.

"It's okay, I can't avoid him forever. Well, I could try."

Lissa and I both laughed at that, and Trace pulled me in for a side hug. "Ready to go?" he asked.

"Yeah." I swung my leg off the side of the table. "It's so much lighter. Thanks, Lissa."

"You're welcome, be sure to call if you have any problems with it."

"I will." Trace put my scooter close enough I just slid onto it and glided out the door. There was enough snow outside I didn't want to chance navigating it, so I waited at the entrance for Trace to bring his truck closer.

"Is your foot cold?" he asked as he got me settled and put away the scooter.

I looked down and noticed my toes sticking out of the end of the cast. "It is. I hadn't even thought about it but yes, if I stub my toe it'll probably pop right off."

He looked at me, turned up the heater, and dissolved into laughter. "Well, we wouldn't want that to happen." He managed to squeak out.

I play slapped at him while he tried to gain control. "You wouldn't be laughing if my toe was laying on the floorboard of your truck."

He froze for a second before busting up in laughter again. "Sorry, I don't know why that sounds so funny to me." He wiped at his eyes and fumbled with his keys.

"I'd really like to keep all ten of my toes if you don't mind. Can we go for a drive through town?"

"I'd like you to keep them all too," he said and leaned in for a quick kiss. "Of course, we can drive around. We can see some of the decorations if you'd like. They're all over town."

"That sounds great. It feels good to be out and not at the airport."

"Did you get to see much of Park City?"

"Some, we drove around when we first got here. Then again when we went out to dinner."

"Well let's give you the dollar tour then. There's a lot you missed."

We drove around the downtown and Trace pointed out all his favorite places to eat or just hang-out. We drove by the outdoor skating rink and watched the skaters slowly make their way around the oval of ice. Trace seemed to wave at every car or truck we passed.

"Does everyone in town know you?"

"Nah, just the skiers. We're a pretty close-knit town and the locals all stick together."

"It sounds nice. We have our little group back home, but Sacramento is quite a bit bigger than Park City. The old part of town has a small-town feel, but it's surrounded by the downtown business area."

"I'll have to go visit it sometime." Trace smiled over at me and patted my leg.

"Yes, you will. I'll show you around."

"I'd like that. Did you want to get something to eat while we're out?"

"Sure, not that I don't appreciate you cooking, but I feel like you need a break. Let me buy you a late lunch."

"I know just the place; do you want to eat there or take it home?"

"Let's eat there. It's about time we went on a date, don't you think?"

"About time? I've known you less than a week and you moved in. We're way beyond dating," Trace said, and rubbed his finger along his lip to hide his smile.

I punched him in the arm, and we both laughed at that. "Oh, my toes. I need a sock." I had forgotten all about my foot for a few minutes, but I didn't think I could sit in a restaurant without anything on my toes. Trace pulled over and rummaged around behind the seats.

"Forgot I had these." He handed me a bundled-up pair of socks. "I usually keep dry socks in the back in case my feet get wet in the snow or water."

"You really are my hero." I reached for the socks and pulled him in for a kiss. There was always time for a kiss.

"How's your leg feeling?"

"So far so good." I shimmied around and pulled a sock onto my toes. "I'm glad I won't have to worry so much about losing a toe."

"Me too, I don't want to have to go back to the medical center any more than is absolutely necessary." He got out of the truck and walked around to my side. I opened the door and waited for him to hand me my scooter.

"Be careful on the snow. I know the streets have been cleared but it's still slippery out here. I don't want you to slip."

"I'll be careful," I said and balanced on my good leg until I could get the scooter worked out with my cast. "Okay I'm ready, let's get some food." I didn't miss that he didn't move from my side, and kept his hands shoved in his pockets. I glided as much as I could onto the sidewalk and up to the door of the nearest restaurant. Trace held the door open for me as I rolled inside.

"Hey, Trace, need a table?" the hostess, an older woman with short blonde hair, asked as she walked toward us holding menus in her hand.

"Yes please. One with room for his leg." He tipped his head my way.

"You got it, this way."

After we were seated and had ordered, I took the time to look around. It had a very warm, homey feeling. The heavy open-beamed ceiling, and what looked like the original wood floor, highlighted the massive fireplace in the middle of the room and all contributed to the welcoming atmosphere.

"So, Trace, tell me more about yourself, where are you from." His smile was slow and warm as he reached for my hand.

"Whatever you want to know, Jordan."

Twenty-One
Digging Deeper

When Jordan asked me to tell him more about myself, I realized I'd been holding him at arm's-length and treating him closer to a patient than someone I'd really like to get to know.

"What do you want to know?"

"Where did you grow up?"

"Not too far from you actually. I grew up in Truckee."

"No way. When did you move away?"

"Right after I graduated high school. I wanted to get away and see more of the country. I drove all over the place for close to a year working odd jobs. In the winter I moved around through the ski areas doing whatever work they needed. After a couple of years, I ended up volunteering for ski patrol in Oregon. I took the classes in my free time to become a paramedic."

"Did you need that training for ski patrol?"

"No, but I had an injury on Mount Bachelor. A young boy, he had a really serious injury, and I wasn't completely sure how to handle it. They only teach us basic first-aid, and a lot of the volunteers are paramedics. My partner that day knew exactly what to do. The kid had gotten out of control and hit a tree, he had a broken pelvis, and had managed to break his nose too. He was only around ten, and when we got to him, he was in a lot of pain and bleeding like crazy. His dad was trying to keep it together for him, but it was pretty bad."

"What did you do? I've heard stories of skiers and boarders being injured, but I've been lucky until this trip."

"My partner guided me through getting him strapped onto a board on the sled to help stabilize him. We got him off the mountain as fast as we could and there was an ambulance waiting at the bottom. He made a full recovery, but he was in rough shape when we got to him."

"You really are a hero," Jordan said as he reached across the table for my hand and squeezed it.

"No, I'm not, I just have good timing." I grinned at him and the warmth in his eyes washed over me as though I was wrapped in a warm fluffy blanket, but it was just him.

My thoughts were interrupted when Maz brought our food. "This looks great, thanks, Maz."

"Sure thing, Trace, if you need anything just wave me over."

"I will." I rubbed my hands together and glanced at Jordan who was looking at me. "What?"

"Nothing, just realizing more and more how amazing you are. And how good this food smells," he said as he picked up a fry and popped it in his mouth with a smile.

We talked between bites, and slowly we found out more and more about each other. Even though we'd spent a few days together, most of the time I'd been focused on his leg. Now I wanted to focus on him and knowing as much about him as I could. He was so easy to be around, fun to talk to, and the more we talked and spent time together, the happier it made me.

"You ready for your bill?" Maz asked as she rushed over from the table next to us.

"Yes please," Jordan said, and pulled out his wallet.

I reached for my own wallet. "Here let me—"

"Don't even think about it." Jordan waved me off without looking up. "It's the least I can do for all you've done for me."

"Well damn, I should have ordered dessert," I joked as he held his credit card out for Maz.

He froze and his eyes met mine again. "What sounds good? We can get it to go and eat it at home if you want?"

I smiled again, I seemed to do that more around him than I had in months. "Maz, what kind of pie do you have today?" She rattled off a list of at least ten different pies and Jordan looked so serious as he was deciding, it would have been easy to believe he was deciding on something far more important than pie.

"I'll take the coconut cream," he said. "What about you, Trace?"

"I'll take the Dutch apple with some ice cream on the side."

"You got it, give me just a minute." Maz hurried over to the kitchen area, and I could feel Jordan's eyes on me. I turned and smiled at him.

"What do you want to do the rest of the day?" I asked.

"Oh, I can think of a few things," he said with a waggle of his eyebrows.

"Maz, we're ready for the check," I said with a wave of my hand as she rushed around getting our order ready. She looked up and rolled her eyes at me.

"Ooooh she told you," Jordan said with a laugh just as she walked over with a bag and handed him his card and the receipt to sign.

"Maz, I didn't introduce you, this is Jordan James. He's going to be staying with me for a little while." Jordan shook her hand and she smiled that smile that said everything she didn't *actually* say. Now it was my turn to roll my eyes.

"Pleased to meet you, Jordan. I hope this one here isn't giving you too much trouble," she said as she pointed her thumb at me over her shoulder.

"Hi, Maz. This guy? He's my hero. He saved my ass when I was stuck up on the mountain."

"Is that right? Well, I guess it's a good thing I gave him an extra piece of pie."

"Thanks, Maz, you didn't have to do that," I said, and took the bag from her.

"I know. But you two are so cute over here giving each other the heart eyes, I couldn't resist. Now go home and enjoy." She picked up the receipt Jordan had signed and moved on to the next table.

"Okay then, let's go," I squeaked out.

Jordan laughed, and moved to his scooter without much trouble. I held the door for him as we left and drew in a deep breath as we moved out into the brisk air. I shoved my hand in my pocket and clenched the bag to stop the urge from touching Jordan one more time. He glided over to the truck and after I unlocked the door, he slid into the seat. "What do you want to do now?" I asked as I put away the scooter.

"I'm ready to go home and watch a movie. How does that sound?" I shut the door and jogged around to the other side. "Sounds good to me. It's too cold out to do much." He reached out for my leg and left his hand there as I drove the short distance to my house. In the back of my mind I knew none of this was permanent, but I didn't want to give those thoughts any time. Not while he was still here.

We pulled up to the house, and I didn't miss Jordan look up at the lights and Christmas decorations. Even though it was still bright out, they were visible. "I really like your house. Have I told you that?"

"Maybe once." I smiled and after parking, got out and walked around to his door. And without even asking I scooped him up and carried him in. He rested his head against my chest, and as I settled him onto the couch, I dreaded leaving him for the short amount of time it would take me to go back out and get our dessert and the scooter. He smiled up at me, and somehow, I think he felt the same way.

"Go on, I'll have your spot all warmed up for you."

I walked back out into the cold and hoped the shock of it would knock some sense into me, but I knew it wouldn't make a difference. I was falling for a man who lived in another state, and who would be going home eventually. Fuck.

Twenty-Two
The Heart Wants

I WATCHED AS TRACE walked back out the door, his reluctance was easy to see in the expression on his face, and the way he rushed out. I understood why. I felt the same way. I knew eventually I'd have to leave, and I wanted to get every little bit of time I could with him.

A crush of emotions hit me like a wave, and made my heart hurt. The thought of not seeing Trace everyday hurt more than I expected it to. I hardly knew him. The time we'd spent together was a blur to me, between being in pain and trying to figure out a new way to do everything with a broken leg, I hadn't put much time into getting to know him. The time at the restaurant was really the first conversation we'd had that didn't revolve around my accident.

"Hey, we got home just in time, it's starting to snow again." Trace walked inside and put the scooter near me before taking off his jacket. He walked into the kitchen with the bag that held dessert. He rubbed his hands together before sitting next to me on the couch. "Are you warm enough?"

"I am now." I snuggled in closer to his side and he pulled me closer.

"Let's see what's on. I'm in the mood to veg out for a while."

"Me too, then we'll eat the yummies," I said, with my head resting on his shoulder.

"Or, we can eat the yummies now." He turned me enough to capture my lips with his. I was lost in the sensations. His tongue swiping across my lips, asking for entry, while his hands wandered all over my arms and back. When we broke apart we were both panting, and I wasn't cold at all.

"Wow," I breathed out. "Every time you kiss me, I never want you to stop." He leaned his head against mine as we caught our breath.

"I have a confession to make. The way I feel with you, I've never felt before. It's like I've always known you. I don't really know how else to describe it. I know we barely know each other, but my heart seems to feel differently."

I turned to face him and took his face in my hands. His eyes looked uncertain, and maybe a little scared. But that wouldn't do, I knew how brave he was. "I feel it too. I know we sort of talked about it at the airport, but maybe we need to talk a little more because I'm not sure I could stand it if I left here without knowing exactly where we stand."

"When do you think you'll be leaving?" he asked, his voice carrying a note of caution.

"I'm not sure, at least another week. Now that I have a cast and the scooter, I feel a little more confident traveling." My mind flashed to being at the airport with Dave and how horrible it was. Feeling vulnerable, and worried about how I'd ever make it on the plane.

"Then let's make the most of the week, and if it turns into more than a week, I'll enjoy every moment of it."

"Promise me you'll say whatever is on your mind while I'm here. Don't hold back. I really want to know everything about you. I promise you won't scare me off, I'm already in deep." It was funny how time, or the lack thereof, seemed to loosen my tongue and I realized it didn't matter. It mattered more that I left and regretted not being honest with him.

"I promise, and I do have a confession."

I took his hand and leaned into his side. "What confession?" I braced myself for the worst, going over our conversation and trying to remember anything he'd said that would have given me a clue, but I came up blank.

He leaned into me and whispered in my ear. "I can't stop thinking about that apple pie."

I froze, he froze, and I gave him a good shove before we both dissolved into laughter. "Oh my god, you scared me to death. I thought you were going to confess something horrible, but I couldn't figure out what the heck it could be."

"Do you mind?"

"If you feed me pie? Hell no, I don't mind. I might want some of your ice cream too."

"Your wish," he said, as he made a rolling motion with his hand before jumping up off the couch. "Sit right there and pick out a movie. I'll get everything ready."

"One more thing," I said as he started to walk away. He raised his brows waiting for me to finish. "This." I pointed at my lips. His smile was beautiful and so full of happiness as he leaned down and smacked my lips. "Thank you, now hurry back." He laughed and hurried to the kitchen. I turned on the television and clicked around trying to decide what to watch. Trace rummaged around in the kitchen and it brought a smile to my face. I'd never thought I'd be one to enjoy sitting at home with a guy and enjoying an afternoon on the couch watching a movie. But there was something so calming about Trace, and his place. This wonderful warm cabin surrounded by snow and filled with more warmth and caring than I'd had in a long time.

"Here ya go," Trace said as he handed me a plate with a piece of coconut cream pie that had to be six inches tall.

"Whoa, they don't play around with their desserts." Trace sat next to me with his Dutch apple pie and a pile of ice cream. "That's a side order of ice cream? It looks like half of a carton."

He shrugged his shoulder and picked up his fork. "Maz knows I like my dessert."

"That smells so good." I leaned closer to him and breathed in the warm cinnamon, caramel, and apple scent. He held a forkful out for me loaded with the gooey goodness. "Mmm so good." One side of his mouth lifted in a grin before he stole a sweet kiss.

We settled on watching *Christmas Vacation* because it never got old. "So, a week . . ." he said without looking at me.

"Yeah, I have to get back to work, and make sure I still have a job to go back to." The pie that had tasted so sweet a moment before, turned to sawdust in my mouth. I didn't want to leave. I wanted to stay here for all the snowy days and cold winter nights. But mostly, I wanted to stay for all the nights with Trace.

Twenty-Three
Sweet Sorrow

AFTER WE FINISHED OUR desserts, sharing bite after bite with each other, Jordan drifted off to sleep, his plate forgotten on his lap. I enjoyed the quiet time, and the opportunity to take in his beautiful features. We were so different in so many ways, including his longer hair, and my short cut. But we had so much in common and what seemed to be a mutual feeling of comfort and companionship in each other's company.

He was so easy to be around. And hot, god was he hot. The long hair made him look edgy, and somehow more stylish in an unplanned way. But his smile, and the way his green eyes lit up whenever he talked about his job, or movies, or anything that he really enjoyed. I leaned close and pressed my lips to his forehead before picking up the plates and taking them into the kitchen.

"How the fuck did this happen?" I mumbled to myself. "When did my damn heart get involved?" Actually, I knew the exact moment. As soon as my eyes locked with his on that ski slope. I shook my head to clear it and walked back to where Jordan now sat leaning in the direction I'd been sitting.

"Come on, cutie," I whispered as I eased him to stretch out and covered him up with the blanket from the back of the couch. Another quick kiss to the forehead and I left him to go out to my workshop.

It seemed so long since I'd been out here, but it had only been a few days. The smell of sawdust and machine oil seemed to permeate the area, and the feeling of familiarity settled into my bones. I picked up where I left off on the skier for the roof, and after I was happy it was sanded smooth, I picked out some paints to add some color to him. A red shirt, black pants, and a yellow helmet.

While the paint dried, I swept up the sawdust, tidied up where I'd painted, and washed the brushes. I'd just turned around to check if the paint had dried when Jordan glided into the shop on his scooter.

"Hey," he said, his voice rough.

"Hey yourself." He rolled right up to me and kissed me before trailing the tip of his nose along my cheek.

"I missed you," he whispered, and pecked my cheek.

I wrapped my arms around him and pulled him close. He smelled so good. My bodywash mixed with pine, and the scent I now knew was all him. "How's your leg?"

"Fine. *Really* fine. I think I'm ready for some activities."

I pulled back and met his eyes. "You want to go out and walk around?"

"Not that kind of activities," he said, with another one of those eyebrow waggles.

I grinned at him, unable to stop myself. "Yeah, what kind of activities are we talking about, Mr. James?" I swayed while pressing my forehead against his.

"Well, you have that huge bed upstairs that we've barely used."

"We've used it. We've slept in it a few times now," I teased.

He met my eyes and brushed the corner of my mouth with his thumb. "You and this damn hot dimple. You have no idea how much I want you, or how much I want everything with you."

I swallowed hard, realizing it was now or never. If I kept my mouth shut, he'd never know. "I feel the same way, and I'd feel like shit if I let you leave and didn't tell you.

Before I met you, my life consisted of working, and coming home to work out here. I didn't realize how much I missed having someone to spend time with."

"I'll be here a while longer," he whispered against my cheek.

"Let's go back inside. I'm done out here, and I don't want to waste any time we have left together."

After checking there was nothing left out or plugged in, I followed Jordan out the door and toward the back door to the house. "Are you hungry?"

"Yeah, but not for food." He turned to face me, and I felt the heat in his gaze. The corner of his mouth lifted in a lopsided grin. "Actually, I think I'm ready for bed."

"But it's not even dark out—oh! You're right, here let me help you." I scooped him up and he laughed as I rushed to carry him up the stairs. His lips met mine just as I turned to settle him on the bed and followed him as he scooted himself up to lean against the headboard. "Is your leg okay?"

"Yes," he breathed out as he kissed my neck. "I'm not even thinking about it right now. I have much more important things on my mind."

I pressed down on him, making sure his cast was well out of the way. Feeling his hardness against my own only made me want to feel even more. He wrapped his uninjured leg around the back of my legs and drew me down to him.

"More," he groaned into my neck.

Reaching over my shoulder, I pulled my sweater and the t-shirt I had under it off at the same time. His hands roamed over my chest and his thumbs brushed at my nipples, making me jerk down on him even more. My hands trailed down his sides and played under the hem of his shirt; my eyes met his asking permission and his nod was all I needed to lift the fabric over his head.

I'd seen him naked a few times, but his body was so lean and toned. Not from a gym but from physical labor. He said he was a mechanic, but apparently, he was a hard worker, and didn't shy away from anything physical. I slid down far enough to lick his abs, making him giggle. "Ticklish?"

"A little." His fingers slid through my short hair and scratched lightly at my scalp, making me shiver for reasons that had nothing to do with the weather. I played with the waistband of my sweatpants that he still wore. His eyes watched me with a dark intensity, waiting to see what my next move would be. My finger glided under the band and he wriggled as much as he could with me pinning him to the bed and wearing a cast.

As I slowly slid his pants down his eyes never left mine, his breathing increased and the sheen of sweat glowed on his forehead. His hard dick sprung free, and it felt like I was seeing him for the first time. The dark pink head begged me to lick it, so I did. Just the tip of my tongue glided over the velvety head and teased at the edge of the frenulum. He groaned and stretched in pleasure.

"Agh," he grunted, and flinched.

"What's wrong?" I shot up off him, and my hands moved not knowing where to check for injuries. "Did I hurt you? Jordan, I'm so sorry. I—"

"Trace, it's fine. When I stretched, I hurt my leg, but it wasn't anything you did. It was just me caught up in the moment and not remembering to be careful. Come back here." He reached out his hand for me, and I moved back between his legs. "Trace, I know you're not the type to hurt anyone on purpose. You're too caring for that."

"You're sure?" I wove my fingers with his and pressed my weight on his uninjured leg.

"I'm so sure. Now what were we doing?" he asked and pulled me closer. "Oh yes, now I remember."

I laughed and gladly obliged, I'd do just about anything he asked, and that was more and more apparent with every passing moment.

Twenty-Four
The Pull

Damn leg. Just when Trace was about to make my dreams come true, my leg had to scream at me for attention.

"Why are you frowning?" Trace asked from where his face hovered just above my dick.

"Just thinking about how my damn leg spoiled the moment."

"Well, I think I have an idea of what could take your mind off it."

"Yes please."

He blew out a laugh and licked me from stump to tip making me flinch away and crave more at the same time.

I stretched back and enjoyed the sensation of his warm mouth on me. He took his time, bringing me to the edge and then pulling me back again. Over and over he did this, until I didn't think I could take it anymore.

"Trace, if you don't back off now, I'm gonna blow." He backed off just a little and blew once again on my tip.

"Isn't that supposed to be the point?"

I cracked my eyes open to see his gaze locked on mine, as he drew me once more into his mouth, and didn't stop until I hit the back of his throat. The sensations overwhelmed me and before I could stop myself, I was shooting down his throat. He licked my now too sensitive dick a few times, before he crawled up next to me.

"Give me a minute and I'll take care of you," I panted out.

"Nope, you just enjoy it, and I'll enjoy snuggling up to you."

I reached my arm behind him as he rested his head on my chest, and I pulled him close to me. My lips brushed over his hair, and with my eyes still closed I imagined this was our life. That I didn't have to leave to go back to Sacramento. But reality slapped me in the face as my phone rang with the ringtone I used for my boss. I tried to jump up, but Trace's weight held me down.

"Trace?"

He laughed and handed me my phone. "Sorry, I had to keep you all to myself for one more minute." And once again I melted.

"Jordan? Answer your damn phone," sounded from the speaker as I swiped it to life and connected the call.

"Lonny, sorry, man. I was going to call you later today."

"How're you doing? Dave didn't know shit, as usual. He said you were staying there. Made it sound like you were staying forever. Is that right?"

My eyes shot to Trace who stood and squeezed my hand before walking toward the bathroom. My eyes followed him, and the farther he got away the more my heart pulled me to follow him.

"Jordan? Did I lose you?"

"Sorry, Lonny, I'm here. I just got a cast today so I'll probably be flying back this weekend."

"That would be great. Do you know if you'll be able to work?"

"They didn't tell me not to. I think as long as I take it easy it'll be fine."

"Sounds good to me. Dave's a good guy but he's not nearly as good a worker as you are. Call me when you get back and I'll put you on the schedule."

"Will do, thanks, Lonny." I hung up and pulled my pants back up from where they were bunched around my knees and swung my legs over the side of the bed. I needed a second to collect my thoughts. I knew I'd have to leave eventually, but I kept hoping something would happen that made it so I could stay.

"Jordan? Did you want to shower?" Trace asked as he stepped out of the bathroom wrapped in a towel.

I didn't feel like smiling, but the hope in his voice made me. "Sure, I'm a little sticky."

"Well come on then. I'll help you wrap your cast, so it doesn't get wet."

He didn't meet my eyes as he guided me to sit on the toilet, helped me remove the sweatpants, and wrapped my cast in a garbage bag. "Trace?" He looked down and secured the bag with some medical tape and paid a little too much attention to what he was doing. "Trace? What is it?" I cupped his cheek and guided his eyes up to meet mine. His hand covered mine, but he still hadn't moved from where he knelt at my feet. Slowly he leaned forward and rested his head on my lap. I combed my fingers through his hair and reveled in the quiet of his house.

"I'm not ready for you to leave," he finally whispered.

"I'm not either. I'm going to miss you more than anything." He had yet to move, so I continued to comb my fingers through his hair. He looked up and his lips met mine. The taste of me was still on his lips, and I pressed my tongue between his lips for one more taste. He pulled back enough to rest his forehead against mine for a moment before he rose and turned on the water in the shower. I stood and balanced the best I could before he was back and helping me slide out of my boxer briefs before guiding me to the shower. We'd done this a couple of times now so we both knew the routine we'd unconsciously established.

He knelt and washed my legs. It was the same as before, except this time I could feel him pulling away emotionally. Building a wall around his heart that I wasn't sure I'd be able to break through. "This doesn't have to be the end you know." At first, he didn't react to my words and just kept washing me. Finally, he paused and lowered his head, before looking up and meeting my eyes.

"I wish that were true. But you have a life in California, and my life is here. I don't see that changing anytime soon."

"I know it's not ideal, but I'd like to try. Give us a chance. Maybe we'll miss each other so much one of us will move, but until then I don't want to lose touch with you. I'll come back and visit you as soon as I can. It's a short flight, I could even come out on a Thursday night and stay until Sunday."

"You'd do that?" His eyes bounced between my own, and he didn't move a muscle as he waited for my answer.

"I'd do that, I'd do just about anything for you."

He blew out the breath he'd been holding, stood and pulled me into his arms. "You'd really do that?"

I grabbed his shoulders and shook him. "Yes! You're worth it, Trace. I'll do whatever it takes."

He smiled then, a real smile. "I'd visit you too. I mean, if you want me to. I get a few days off at once, so if you wanted me to, I could spend maybe three or four days at a time."

I took his face in my hands and looked deep into those beautiful intelligent eyes. "I want that, I want that more than I can put into words. I don't want to let you go, and if that means we fly every other month or every other weekend, I'm willing to do that. For you."

He settled his hand over mine and neither of us moved, content just to be in each other's company surrounded by warm water and steam.

Twenty-Five
The Plan

The emotions that burned through me when I imagined Jordan gone were soul destroying. I was at a loss for how this man, that I hadn't known existed a few weeks ago, was now the number one person in my world. We stayed in the shower until the water started to run cold, and I realized we hadn't gotten anything clean except for Jordan's legs and his foot.

"Let's just go sit on the couch and snuggle. I want to spend as much time together as we can. I need to get another ticket to go home, but I'm trying not to think about it too much."

"That sounds good. And you know tomorrow is New Year's Eve," I said, going for nonchalant but hoping for more affect.

"Is it? I totally forgot. We got here the day after Christmas and with everything that's happened, I haven't even thought about the holiday."

"We could go out—I mean, if you want to. Or we could stay in. Or—" Jordan pressed his finger to my lips as we sat in the bedroom both in different degrees of dress.

"Let me handle it. You've taken care of every meal so far. Let me do this. I'm happy to stay in if you are. What do you think?" He talked fast in a way I now knew meant he was excited.

I kissed him and held his face with both hands. "If I can spend the night with you, I'll be happy." His eyes were warm and filled with emotions I didn't want to start to figure out. But I wanted him to keep looking at me like that.

"There's nothing I want more," I whispered. "But first, I think we need to get dressed." He laughed at that, and I dug out two pairs of flannel pajama pants and t-shirts for us to settle into.

"I need to do some laundry," Jordan said as he dug into his suitcase that looked like it mostly held clothes he'd already worn.

"I can start a load. Pull out whatever you want washed." He made a pile that was most of what was inside his suitcase. "Is that all of it?"

"Yeah, are you sure you don't mind?" he asked.

"Why would I mind? Let me take you downstairs and I'll start the laundry." Without waiting for an answer, I scooped him up and carried him down to the couch. With a quick kiss I ran back up and gathered up the laundry. With another quick kiss and a laugh as I passed him, I rushed off to start the laundry.

When I walked back into the living room, he was on the couch holding a pad of paper and tapping a pen against his lips.

"What have you got there?"

He smiled and tapped the pen on his lips like he'd done earlier. "Just making a list."

"Oh really." I leaned in close and tried to look but he leaned away and clutched it to his chest.

"No peeking, I want it to be a surprise."

"Oh, sounds fun. Promise you'll tell me if you need me to do anything. I don't mind at all."

"Trace, I want to do this for you. I'll let you know if I need any help. And thanks for asking." He kissed me on the cheek and went back to writing and tapping and making sure I couldn't see what he was writing. I remembered what he'd written in the back of that notebook, the words that had given me the courage to drive to the airport. I pulled him to me and kissed him until we both pulled apart and panted for lack of oxygen. "Wow, I don't know what got into you, but more of that please. Wait, not right now though. I need to finish this." He shoved me and went back to writing.

I picked up the remote and turned the television on and scrolled to see what piqued my attention. There was an older Warren Miller ski movie on, so I chose that. Soon enough Jordan's eyes were no longer on his list and were now on the television. "Have you watched any of these?" I asked.

"No, I've heard of them though."

"These guys are crazy. But they're such good skiers and you can tell they're having the time of their lives." We were quiet for a while just watching different groups of skiers plow down through chest deep snow from steep mountain tops.

"Can you ski like that? I can't even imagine it."

"Yeah, I've skied for years, and done a bit of backcountry and heli-skiing."

"No shit? I've skied for a while, but I never seem to get much better. I'm happy on the intermediate trails. Much less chance that I'll end up injured." He laughed and snuggled closer to me. "Not like I'll be skiing anytime soon."

"Yeah, this season's out for sure. But you'll have next year. I'm sure by then you could go if you took it easy."

"I always take it easy," he said without taking his eyes off the skiers on TV. I hoped by next year we'd be able to ski together. And if we weren't skiing at least we'd be together. Because I wasn't kidding when I told him I didn't want him to leave, and right now I wanted to remember him exactly as he was. Snuggled in next to me with a look of wonder on his face one moment, and a happy smile the next. There had to be a way for us, there just had to be.

Twenty-Six
New Year's Eve

My list was done. I'd called and placed orders for the food and drinks. I had planned to rent one of the new release movies, but then I thought it might be nice to have a more intimate evening with candlelight and music. I thought about it for a moment and realized we both really loved sitting there watching movies. It didn't really seem to matter what movie it was as long as we were there together.

"I'm going to go into work and just make sure they don't need me for anything. Will you be okay here for a while, or did you want to go?"

"Go ahead, now that I have my scooter, I'm fine. Plus, it gives me time to finalize some of my plans for later."

He sat next to me on the couch and took my hand in his. "Are you sure? I can always call and check. It's just with the holiday we sometimes get overwhelmed."

"Yeah, I'm sure. Go ahead, I'll be fine. I've got everything I need right here, and I can call if I need you. It's not like you'll be far."

"I won't be long, I promise." He kissed me as he rose off the couch. "I just want to make sure they're completely stocked with supplies and ready for anything."

"Is that normally your job?" I asked, realizing I didn't know much about what he did.

"Yes, I usually keep track of all our supplies, and everyone's schedule. It's not as though the others can't do it, but I'll worry if I don't go and see for myself that everything is taken care of."

"I totally understand, go ahead so you can hurry back to me." I wasn't sure what made me say that, but I smiled when I let myself admit it was true. I missed him already and he wasn't even out the door. With a blast of cold air, and a wave good-bye, I was alone.

It was mid-afternoon and still too early for dinner, but I called the places I'd ordered from to see if they could bring everything over now. I wanted to make this night special. We had one more night after this, but my plane left early, so this would be the last night we could spend the whole night together and not worry about getting up in the morning.

The restaurant was more than happy to have the order ready early, and promised it would be here within the hour; the other places were just as accommodating, and before too long I was answering the door and letting in the visitors who would make our night complete.

"Do you need any help?" one of the delivery people asked. She was a few years younger than me, and probably working for some extra money.

"I think I got it. But thank you." She waved as she walked out the door, and after closing it behind her I got to work on setting everything up.

If Trace was anything like me there was no way he'd get out of work as fast as he expected. Every time I dropped in I got busy talking to one of the other mechanics, or got interested in someone's project. I knew he loved his job, which was why he insisted on going to check everything was running smoothly while he had the week off.

He had a heart of gold that was easy to see. I thought back to when he'd said we'd make it work and I hoped we could. I wanted to fight for him. He was so special, and I wanted to see where our relationship could go. But right now, I wanted to surprise him.

I plated the food and wrapped it up in foil so I could keep it warm in the oven. After I was sure everything would be perfect with the food, I took the chocolate cake out of the box and set it on a plate. After scooting around and gathering a few candles, I set them up on the counter next to the cake to set the mood a bit. The flowers I'd bought were next. I rummaged around for a vase, but when I couldn't find one, I settled for a coffee can. It actually gave it a nice rustic look that suited his cabin. All that was left was for me to pick a couple of movies and have them ready to go.

I looked around at what I'd accomplished and hoped it gave a little bit of magic to his house. I still didn't understand why he had no decorations. He obviously loved the holiday. I knew he liked to share the lights with everyone else, but he needed to have a nice holiday welcome when he returned home. The candles didn't exactly make it look like Christmas lights, but they gave everything a warm glow.

Hearing his truck pull up out front, I settled onto the couch. He rushed inside the door, then froze when he saw the candles. His eyes moved around the room, taking in the cake, and flowers, before finally landing on me. His smile was so big and bright, I couldn't help but smile right back at him.

"Jordan, what's all this?" He looked down where he still held the door handle and turned to close it.

"Surprise, I wanted tonight to be special. I hope you don't mind." I held my arms out to him, and he rushed to me.

"You did all this? But how? I thought you'd have dinner delivered but I never thought you'd do all this."

"You're worth it all. I wanted us to have a night to remember."

"Every night with you is a night to remember," he said, before kissing me.

I pulled back and held his face in my hands. "Go change into your comfy clothes and we'll go ahead and eat if you're ready." He gave me a look that said hell yes, he was ready. With a quick kiss to the cheek he ran upstairs, and after some shuffling around, and drawers being opened and closed, he was back downstairs, and holding his hand out to me.

"Come on, show me what you've been up to."

As soon as I stood, he scooped me into his arms and walked me over to one of the stools that faced the kitchen. "Okay, first thing, open the oven."

He complied and once he peeked under the foil, turned to me with a grin. "I knew you were my favorite." He rubbed his hands together before using a towel to pick up both plates and set them on the bar.

"Well, come on, let's get started. This smelled so good I almost didn't want to wait."

"You know you'd always wait for me." He said it as a joke, but I knew it was true. There was something about him that made me want to wait. I just hoped I didn't lose that feeling in the next few months. Because either way, soon enough we'd know if there was enough between us to wait for.

Twenty-Seven
A Night to Remember

We both peeled back the foil from our plates and to my delight there was a variety of barbecued meats: tri-tip, baby-back ribs, and chicken. Along with beans and a couple of slices of home-baked bread. "Is this from—"

"The barbecue place just down the road? Yes, we ate there the first night we were here, and it was so good. I was hoping it was one of your favorites."

"Well you thought right, thank you, Jordan. This is all great." He grinned at me, and after I got us both drinks—beer for me and seltzer water for him—we both wasted no time digging into all the great tasting food.

"So, what are your resolutions for the new year?" Jordan asked as he wiped sauce from his cheek.

"I don't usually make resolutions. How about you?"

"No, not usually. I try to set a goal and hope to accomplish it. But sometimes that doesn't work out either."

"So how are things at your job?"

"It's good, I've worked there so long I feel like it's all I know. It's gotten to be pretty routine. We do have those jobs that are above the ordinary though, and those are a lot of fun. Someone wanting to customize their car or truck. I love that shit, it's so much more fun than an oil change." He smiled and went back to eating for a moment, before he asked, "What about you? Do you want to do ski patrol much longer?"

"I want to do it as long as I can. I love everything about it, and when there's no snow and I work as a paramedic, I love that too."

"Sounds like you have the best of both worlds."

"I think so. It's never dull that's for damn sure."

"So, what made you stick with Park City? I know you said you'd worked at a few different places."

I took a drink of beer and paused to collect my thoughts. I moved here for a specific reason, and even though I'd never told anyone exactly what that reason was, I knew telling Jordan would help him understand me, not drive him away. "I didn't know anyone here. When I left the place in Washington, I decided I needed to start living how I wanted to live. Nothing bad happened there, but I wasn't living as honestly as I should have been. No one there knew I was gay. I doubt any of them would have cared. But I'd hidden it for so many years, I wasn't sure how to come out to them. So, I left instead, and decided I'd start over and live my life the way I was meant to."

He turned and faced me. "I cannot even imagine how hard that had to be for you."

"Don't get me wrong, it wasn't like I was being harassed or anything. It was just me being stuck, and not knowing how to move forward."

"Well, then I'm glad it all worked out for you. It seems like you have a good group of friends here. I mean except Dr. Ex," he said with a smirk.

"Oh god, don't remind me." I buried my face in my hands. Why was I ever so stupid to even consider going out with him?

Jordan peeled my fingers away from my face and smiled before he kissed me again. "I'm glad he's your ex. Just sayin'."

We finished eating while sharing smiles and bumping shoulders. He rubbed his stocking-clad foot against mine which distracted me in ways it really shouldn't have. It was then I really took notice of the flowers. A beautiful mixed bouquet with roses and other flowers I didn't know the names of. "Did you order these?" I asked as I stepped over to where they were placed on the counter in a coffee can.

"Possibly."

"Possibly?"

"If you like them then they were from me. If you're not a flower guy, then I have no idea what asshole sent them."

I burst out laughing, and watched his smile grow even more before I stalked over to him. A look passed over his features that sort of looked like he thought about running but then realized he would have to hop. I stood between his legs and held his face in my hands as I stroked my thumb over his lips. "I'm a flower guy. I love them."

"Did I mention there's dessert?" Jordan whispered between kisses.

"No, I'm pretty sure I would have remembered that."

"Chocolatey goodness," he murmured.

"Oh god, the things you say." I fake swooned. But maybe it wasn't totally fake, I wasn't one to say no to dessert especially chocolate.

"It's right over there," he said and turned my face toward the counter he'd set it on. He'd placed a few candles around the place, and I had to admit, it gave everything a warm glow. I walked over and cut a slice of the rich chocolate cake and placed it on a plate.

"I think maybe I can help you with this," I said as I walked back to where I'd been between his legs. I scooped up a bite of cake and offered it to Jordan. His eyes locked with mine as he slowly pulled his lips from the fork and groaned.

"That is so good—"

Before he could finish his sentence, my lips were on his, and both of us groaned. "So, good," I agreed.

"Trace, I have a confession."

"What is it?" I was worried, he sounded so serious and I went over the last few moments in my mind but couldn't recall anything I'd said or done that might have been taken in the wrong way.

"I want you so bad right now."

His eyes darkened as the words left his mouth, and I felt my own heartrate speed up.

"But I really feel like there's something more between us than just sex. And I want to take our time and not rush anything. Trace, you're important to me."

I brushed his hair back from his brow and tucked it behind his ear. "I feel it too. I've always felt it. And I'd really like us to take our time exploring all these feelings. I want to make it important. Make *us* important. Does that make sense?"

His smile was gentle as he traced his fingers along my brow. "I love this face," he whispered, and I wasn't sure he realized what he'd said before he leaned in to kiss me. "We'll make it work. And we'll spend the time we're apart getting to know each other even more. We'll be okay," he soothed, and the gentle tone of his voice flowed over me and calmed my frazzled nerves. We'd make it, one way or another, it would happen.

Twenty-Eight
Everything Changes

The night flew by so fast. One minute Trace was walking in the door, and a few hours later the clock struck midnight. We watched the countdown on television, after watching an action movie I'd rented. I'd poured us both a glass of champagne from the bottle I'd ordered along with dinner.

"I'm not much for champagne," Trace had said with a shy smile that was far from his normal confident self.

"Me either, and I know I shouldn't be drinking since I can't stand on my own. But I really wanted to make a toast tonight." I held my glass out to his and clinked them.

"To us, and all the future holds. Happy New Year, Mister Griffin."

"Happy New Year, Mister James."

After a few sips, Trace turned off the lights and we watched the snow fall silently through the big windows at the front of the house. Snuggled on his couch with him, watching the feathery snow drift down on a background of night. A few fireworks sounded and we both jumped at the sound.

"It's at the resort, they put on a big show every New Year's."

"We'll have to go sometime," I said, and snuggled in closer. He kissed the top of my head.

"Sometime, but right now there's no place else I'd rather be."

A thought flashed through my mind for split-second. Thoughts of us lying in bed, and finally having sex. But in my mind, I switched that to making love. Trace pulled me close, and my eyes drifted closed. It was a good night, and even better company. And if waiting made us want each other that much more, it was a risk I was willing to take.

I awoke a few hours later when the sun was just starting to stream in through the big windows. Trace had shifted us, so we were now side by side on the couch with my leg on the edge, so I didn't end up hurting it in my sleep.

"Trace? Are you awake?" He jerked awake and looked at me before pulling me close.

"I'm so glad you're still here. I thought I'd slept through it all and you'd left already."

"Nope, but today I should make sure I have everything taken care of. My flight tomorrow is so early I won't have time in the morning for anything."

"I'm driving you," he said, now fully awake. "Is there anything you want to do today?"

"No, I just want to spend time with you. If that's okay?"

"I can't think of anything I'd rather do."

♦♦

The day passed by far quicker than I would have liked. Trace had done my laundry, so I packed up all my things that had ended up scattered around his bedroom and bath. He stayed downstairs while I did this and kept busy in the kitchen.

I was finally able to get around with one crutch, but the scooter was far easier, and I was so glad I'd have it at the airport. Without thinking, I slumped on the bed and looked around Trace's bedroom and out over the balcony. I'd miss this place, and I'd miss him.

My phone sounded with a text interrupting my maudlin thoughts.

Get down here.

I smiled; he was so subtle—not really—but so sweet.

Who is this? I typed back.

"You know who it is," he yelled up the stairs just before I heard him rushing up them. "Are you all ready?"

"Yeah, I'm going to miss this place. It's so comfortable here, makes me feel like I'm home." He sat on the bed next to me and took my hand in his.

"I'm glad you feel that way. It won't be the same without you."

"What do you think about flying out to Sacramento? Maybe in a few weeks you could come out and see where I live. I mean, if you want to."

"I'd love to. I didn't want to come off as pushy and invite myself. Are you sure you don't mind?"

"I'm sure. And if I know I'll see you soon, it'll make leaving a little easier."

"I never thought I'd meet someone on the mountain. I actually never thought I'd meet anyone who I clicked with."

"Well, now you're stuck with me. If you don't come and visit me, I'll be back here looking for you." I meant it as a joke, but the hope in his eyes betrayed his true feelings.

"I'll find you. Don't even think once you leave here, I won't be waiting for your phone call telling me you arrived. When I go back to work, I'll check with management and see when I can take a few days off. I like the idea of going there on Thursday and coming back on Sunday."

I kissed him that thought made me so happy. "I'd like that so much. Let me know the date and I'll take that Friday off... Trace? Thank you." I took his hand and wove our fingers together.

"We got this," he whispered, before kissing me again.

The rest of the day was spent ignoring the fact we only had a few more hours left. We played a few games, ate cake and other leftovers, and I tried as hard as I could not to watch the clock. But by the time it was nine o'clock I was having trouble keeping my eyes open. The late night and early morning had caught up with me.

"Come on, baby, let's get you upstairs," Trace whispered to me as he scooped me up. I clung to him as much as I could, but the lack of sleep left me groggy and weak. "Don't worry, I've got you."

He whispered something else, but I was already asleep. Left only with the memory of his voice, but no knowledge of what he'd said, and heartbroken that once again time seemed to be against us.

Twenty-Nine
From A Distance

The drive to the airport ended far too soon. Why was it when I drove out here to pick up a friend, or to drop one off, it seemed to take forever? Not today—traffic seemed to part as soon as we were on the freeway, and we made it there with time to spare.

"Looks like you'll have time to relax before your plane leaves." I squeezed Jordan's hand and glanced at him as he looked out the window. It was still dark out. His plane would leave just as the sun was starting to rise, and he'd take a piece of my heart with him.

"Yeah, I hope it's on time."

"Are you ready to go back to work?"

"Not really. I mean, I miss the work, and I miss the guys. But—"

He didn't have to say another word. I understood. I thought I'd be happy being alone and doing what I wanted to do with my life. But the past few days had shown me how wrong I'd been. "I know. I know exactly how you feel. I feel it too." He still hadn't looked at me, but he leaned across the console as much as he could and pulled my arm close to him.

"I'll miss you," he whispered.

Emotions filled me, and I couldn't have answered if I wanted to. And fuck if I didn't find a place as soon as I pulled into the airport. Fate was not on our side today. I helped him with his scooter and carried his suitcase.

"You're checking this, right?" I asked, as we made our way to the Southwest counter.

"Yeah, I have enough to deal with without trying to wrestle it into the overhead compartment." We walked in, and this time I wasn't surprised that there were only a few people in line ahead of us.

"I'll stick around until you go to your gate. I can't leave you yet."

"I'd like that."

"Next please," the agent said, and urged us forward. She was tiny, maybe twenty years old, and I wondered how she handled the heavy bags. "I'll need your ID and ticketing information."

Jordan put everything on the counter without a word.

"Did you want to check your bag?"

"Yes please, he broke his leg so there's no way he could deal with a bag."

"Oh no, let me see what I can do. Did that happen while you were here?" she asked as she tapped away on her keyboard.

"Yeah, took a run I shouldn't have."

"And did your friend here go down it too?"

"No, he saved me."

She stopped typing then and looked between the two of us. "For real?"

"Yep, my handsome ski patrol guy." Jordan grinned at me, and I had to force myself not to kiss him.

"Well thank goodness you weren't hurt any worse. I can get you early boarding, and they'll help you once you're on the plane." She looked over the counter at his scooter. "Gate check your scooter and they'll have it waiting for you when you get off the plane in Sacramento."

"Thank you. Oh, how much to check my bag?" he asked as she slapped tags on it and flung it onto the conveyer belt.

"Nothing, I thought you needed a break." She grinned at that and Jordan barked out a laugh and shook his finger at her. She smiled and called the next person forward.

"Let's get a coffee before you go to your gate." I led us to one of the many vendors available before he'd go through TSA and to his gate.

"That sounds so good. I feel like I could fall back asleep if I sit too long."

"Well let me get you some caffeine to get you on your flight. You can sleep all the way to Sacramento."

"Can I just say I am so glad I booked a non-stop flight. I think I only have one boarding left in me." He laughed at that, but I could tell he wasn't joking.

"Let them help if you need it. Hopefully your flight won't be too crowded." I looked around at the crowd of people everywhere around us, rushing to who knew what.

"I will. Don't worry, I'll make it there."

"Is someone picking you up at the airport?"

"No, I'll just call for a car. It's less complicated that way, and I can get home faster than waiting to see who has time to come and pick me up."

"I wish I could be there to take you home. I'd like to be there to help you if you need it." It was killing me to let him fly by himself, and not know how he'd even get home. I knew it was easy enough to call for a car, but the need in me to keep him safe made me even more nervous about his flight.

He squeezed my hand as we sat at a small table next to a coffee shop. "I know. That's what makes you you. Always ready to help."

"Yeah well, you aren't wrong, but you're not just anybody to me. Stay right here and I'll get us a coffee." I stood and walked away before I said something that scared him away. The urge to look out for him had only grown with the extra time we'd spent together.

I ordered us both a coffee along with two toasted bagels. When I walked back to where he sat I stood for a moment and gazed at him while he wasn't aware I was looking. He was everything I didn't know I wanted, and then some. And now he was leaving. I stumbled forward to the table feeling a little off kilter.

"Thanks," Jordan said with a smile.

"Anytime." He looked up at me and squinted his eyes before he reached for my hand and kissed the back of it.

"Trace, we got this. Don't worry, this isn't the end."

"I hope you're right because right now it feels like I'm getting ready to tear my heart in half so you can take part of it with you. I mean—" I shook my head and looked down at the floor knowing exactly how stupid that sounded.

He reached over and guided my face up until he could meet my eyes. "I'm leaving part of my heart here with you, so maybe together we'll be able to make them both whole again," he whispered, all humor gone from his eyes.

We sipped the coffee, and I tried to force down the bagel that had turned to sawdust in my mouth.

"That's me," he said as he looked at one of the multiple flight boards. His flight was early. *What a surprise.* He stood and balanced on the chair while I threw away our trash and helped him get settled on his scooter. I rested my hand on his back and followed him to the line that would take him through TSA. I walked with him until the agent at the entry gave me a look that said I couldn't go any farther.

We turned to face each other standing off to the side, and I squeezed his hand. "I guess this is as far as I can go. Have a safe flight."

"I'll call you as soon as I land in Sacramento."

"Yes, let me know you've made it."

"I will."

We stared at each other for what was probably way too long, but I didn't give a fuck. I wanted to remember everything about him. "Bye, Jordan," I whispered.

Thirty
A Hurt So Deep

Trace watched as I made my way slowly through the TSA line. The distance between us already was too far. Every time I stumbled with the scooter Trace lurched forward. I knew it was hard on him standing there watching and not being able to help, but it would have been worse if he'd left. At least for me.

I made it through the line to the X-ray machine, and after they checked out my scooter, I was through on the other side. I looked for Trace but didn't see him through the crowd. Turning to go on to my gate I noticed something out of the corner of my eye. When I looked again, I saw him jump up just enough to see him over the crowd.

He waved and I laughed. This guy! I waved back before turning to scoot to my gate.

Getting on the plane took some patience, and a little help from one of the flight attendants. But once I was settled in, I slept all the way to Sacramento, and dreamed of a man that held me close and made me feel safe.

We landed in Sacramento early, and once again I needed help to get off the plane. Riding the tram back to the terminal wasn't all that fun either, but while I waited for my suitcase, I took my phone out to call Trace. Dead. Why didn't I charge it? Of all the times I needed it this was one of the most urgent.

"Can I help you with something?" a man with an airport uniform asked, as he stood in front of a luggage carousel organizing bags and other items as they appeared on a conveyor belt.

"I'm not sure. I need to call for a ride, but my phone is dead." I shook it at him to show him.

"There's a charging station there," he pointed, before he walked off to help someone else. I waited for my bag, and after struggling to lift it off the carousel I pulled up the handle and with a little trial and error I pulled it over to the charging station. There was a chair available, so I sat down and dug through my suitcase for my charger. Cursing myself the whole time.

After twisting around as much as my cast would allow, throwing my clothes all over the floor, and sweating profusely with the effort, finally, I found the fucking charger in the bottom corner of my bag. I ripped it out of there, then checked that I hadn't damaged it. That would be just my luck today. I plugged it in then my phone into it. It was so dead all I got was the empty battery symbol. Fuck. My. Life.

My leg bounced as I waited for it to be charged enough to call for a ride. There was a bank of phones located near the exit that were for shuttles, but I wasn't sure I could call for a ride from them, so I sat with all of my patience gone, and bounced my leg a bit more.

I was interrupted from my thoughts when my phone started going off with texts and emails, and possibly a voicemail or two. I scooted as close as I could and stretched the cord so it was still plugged in and I could go through all the notifications.

There were a few texts from the guys at work welcoming me back, and multiple emails. I closed all those alerts and opened the ride app before something else happened and I couldn't order a car. It estimated a twenty-minute wait, so I let the phone charge a few more minutes while I shoved everything back in my bag. After struggling to get it closed again, I stood and used my scooter to balance as

I unplugged my phone and tucked the cord away where I could get to it a little easier if I needed to.

The scooter made moving a lot easier, but the crowds of people made it that much tougher. As soon as I made it through the doors and checked my phone for a message from the driver, a car pulled up.

"You waiting for a ride?"

"Yes, are you my driver?"

"I am if you're Jordan James." He smiled and opened the door. "Here, you look like you could use a hand."

"You have no idea," I mumbled as I gladly let him take my suitcase and put it in the trunk.

"Go ahead and get in, I'll get that," he said, with a wave at the scooter.

I slid into the back seat and blew out a deep breath. Fuck what a trip. There was a charger cord on the backseat and just as I was about to ask if it was okay to use, he told me there was a charger, and a plug, and if I needed anything else to ask.

My eyes slid shut as we drove away from the airport.

"We're here," the driver said.

I blinked and rubbed my eyes and realized I was back in my own neighborhood. No snow, no bright Christmas lights or cute cutouts, nothing of what I'd left just this morning. Nothing of Trace to be found.

The driver pulled the car into the driveway and was out and opening the trunk before I had time to try to get out of the back seat. As soon as I stood, he was there with my scooter and my suitcase.

"Do you need help getting inside?"

"No, I can make it." I silently hoped that was true and I didn't need to call someone else to help me. I scooted up the driveway to the door. Fucking stairs. There were only two but enough to slow me down.

"Don't forget this," the driver jogged over to me waving my phone at me.

"Oh god, thank you so much."

"Here, let me get that." Without waiting for me to answer, he lifted my suitcase up the stairs and turned to do the same with the scooter. I balanced on one leg and hoped I could make it up two stairs on my own. As I was trying to figure out how I was going to, he must have noticed my hesitance because he held his hand out.

"Thank you so much. I'm still trying to figure out how to get around in this thing."

"No problem. My brother broke his leg when we were kids and needed a lot of help."

"What's your name?" I asked. He'd been more than nice to me and I felt I at least needed to put a name to the face.

"Craig Bailey, it's on the app. If you need a lift again you can request me."

I settled my leg back on the scooter and unlocked my door. "I might just take you up on that. Thanks again, Craig, I appreciate all your help."

He walked toward his car with a backwards wave and drove off. He was maybe a little older than me, his head was shaved but it didn't diminish his striking good looks, if anything it added to them. But he was no Trace. Trace! Fuck I needed to call him. I pushed the door open and flung my suitcase in. The house was cold, but it wasn't empty. The tinkling of a dog tag and the shuffling of paws told me Hunter, my Labrador retriever, knew I was home.

"Hey, boy," I called as he lumbered over to me, head down, tail wagging, and a happy doggie grin on his face. "Sorry I was gone so long. I hope Grandma took good care of you."

"Of course I took good care of him, I was just coming over to feed him. Now, care to tell me what happened?" My mom stood just outside the door, arms crossed, tapping her foot with a look that went between concerned and pissed.

"Yep, come on in. Get comfortable, it'll take a while." Mom and Dad lived a few blocks over. Close enough to be here in a few minutes, but far enough to give me a little privacy.

She walked in, looked at my leg, rolled her eyes, and went right to the kitchen. "I can tell I'll need coffee for this one."

I was beginning to think this day needed more than just coffee, but that probably wouldn't end well either.

Thirty-One
Worry

I WENT RIGHT HOME after I'd left Jordan in the line for TSA. I waited as long as I could but when he'd made it through the X-ray machine, I knew I wouldn't be able to see him anymore. The drive home seemed to take a lot longer than the drive in had, and when I pulled up to my house, I knew I should have gone somewhere else to keep my mind off Jordan.

I checked my phone, but I knew it was way too early for him to call, and when I walked inside the silence was deafening. I'd always enjoyed the quiet solitude here, but already I missed having Jordan here to greet me when I came home. Time for me to go out to the workshop. At least out there I could keep myself busy, and I wouldn't mind the silence or the loneliness.

Because one thing was certain, I was lonelier than I'd realized before I met Jordan. Or maybe just meeting someone I connected with had felt so good I couldn't get enough of that feeling? Either way, I missed him, and he'd only been gone a few hours. I didn't take the time to change my clothes, just walked right through to the door that led to what I hoped kept my mind busy until he called.

♦♦

I'd nearly finished mounting all the lights on the skier when my phone rang. I dropped everything and lunged for it, barely keeping it from flying out of my hands before I could gain control of it and answer.

"Hello?"

"Hey, Trace, I just wanted to check that you were still okay to work tomorrow."

"Brad? Yeah, I'm planning on it."

"Are you out of breath?"

"I was rushing to get the phone and almost dropped it."

"Okay, I thought maybe your guy was still there."

"My—oh no he left earlier. I thought it was him calling."

"Tell me all about it tomorrow. I'll see you bright and early."

"Sounds good, see you then." I hung up and after I checked the time, I checked my phone once again to make sure I hadn't missed a message or text from Jordan. Nothing. I debated calling him, but I didn't want to bother him if he was having a tough time. After deciding to wait a while longer, I walked back into the house, jogged up the stairs to the bedroom and froze.

Funny how fast I'd gotten used to him being there. I'd tripped over his suitcase many times the past week, and now it looked so empty in the space on the floor it had occupied. I stripped off my clothes and when I tossed them in the laundry basket, I noticed one of Jordan's shirts. I picked it up and breathed him in, my eyes closed, and I remembered his smile, and the twinkle he always seemed to have in his eyes even when he was going through a lot of shit.

How the hell was I going to get through the next month without seeing him? I set his shirt down on my bed and walked into the bathroom. He'd left a few of his things here too. A bottle of shampoo, his toothbrush, and some floss. I tucked them all away in the cabinet. He'd be back. And when he was, I hoped it was for longer. But even if it wasn't, I'd have his things here when he returned.

After showering and shaving, I walked back into the bedroom with my towel wrapped around my waist. My phone lit up on the bed, and I swiped it to life.

Sorry I'm so late. You'll never believe the day I've had. Call me when you can xo.

Relief flooded through me, and I dialed his number before I'd consciously decided to do so.

"Hello?"

"Jordan, did you make it home safe?"

"I made it to my house, but I'm not sure it feels like home anymore." His words wrapped around me, and a grin I couldn't control made it hard for me to speak.

"I know the feeling," I whispered. "It's not the same without you here."

"I'm so sorry I didn't call you sooner. My phone was dead when I landed, and I had a tough time getting to a charging station so I could charge it enough to call for a ride."

"Oh no, babe, I'm sorry. I should've offered to fly out with you." The thought of him being stuck without his phone and alone worried me almost as much as him flying by himself with a broken leg.

"It's not your fault. I should have made sure I charged it. I guess I forgot to plug it in last night."

"I'm glad you made it home safe. I've been worried since I last saw you in the TSA line."

"That part of the trip was fine. I slept all the way to Sacramento, and again in the car to my house."

"Are you all settled in at your house?"

"Yeah, me and Hunter are kicked back on the couch."

"Hunter?" I racked my brain to remember that name but couldn't come up with anything.

"My dog. I thought I told you about him."

"No, not that I remember. I'm glad you're not there alone."

"My mom was here earlier. She's been taking care of him while I was gone. She snuck over on an intel mission to get all the dirt about my vacation."

I laughed at that. "Was there dirt?"

"Well according to her there was. Or I was hiding something, or I don't even know. She was here as soon as I had the door unlocked and just left right before I messaged you."

"Sounds fun." He was silent for a moment, and I realized I'd been smiling the whole time we'd been talking.

"I can think of a few things that are more fun."

"I can think of a few things with you that are more fun. Even if we're just sitting on the couch watching movies."

"I liked that. Trace—"

"Yeah, Jordan?" He was silent for a beat too long and I checked that we hadn't been disconnected.

"I really miss you."

"I know, baby, I feel the same way. When I'm at work tomorrow I'll find out how soon I can get a weekend off."

"That would be great. Because I don't think I want to go too many weekends without seeing you."

His bare honesty killed me. How the hell had I let him leave?

"Me either, Jordan. We got this." I hoped I sounded confident, but deep inside I knew nothing was for sure, and he might meet someone else who lived right there and made him forget me, but I hoped that didn't happen. And I made a promise to make sure I somehow got to Sacramento as soon as possible.

Thirty-Two
Time Drags On

THE FIRST WEEK I was back the days were long and I was so tired by the time I got home I fell asleep on the couch before I had time to eat dinner. Hunter kept me company, seeming to realize I needed him more than I normally did. He was a big loveable lug and was always very friendly. But now he was always at my side. My mom came over whenever she was in the area to check on me. I had to admit it was kinda nice knowing I had people around me that cared.

Work was a whole new world. I couldn't do as much as I hoped. The cast was just high enough to give me limited mobility, and if I had to get under a car to work . . . well, that wasn't happening.

"How was work?" Trace asked a few weeks later.

"Fine, I can't do too much so it's almost not worth going in. But if I sit here all day, I'll lose my mind."

"Well, maybe I can keep you occupied."

I sat up on the couch not wanting to miss a word. "What do you have in mind?"

"What's your address?"

"Why do you ask?"

"Just trust me, what's your address."

I paused, but then I rambled off the information. What would it hurt? He covered the phone and I heard a muffled conversation before he was back on the line.

"What are you up to?" I asked, but he distracted me by telling me all about how much it had snowed, and how many rescues they'd already had this week.

"We had to do some avalanche prevention this morning. The snow came in so heavy we were worried about it causing problems in the bowl."

"Oh wow, really glad I didn't know that was a thing when I was there. I was already scared enough without worrying about an avalanche."

"We won't worry about that until next year."

I could hear the smile in his voice, and it gave me a warm feeling sitting there talking to him. We chatted away just like we did when we were on his couch, and I closed my eyes and imagined that's where I was. Hunter jumped up and jogged to the door just before the doorbell rang.

"Hold on, someone's at the door."

"Okay."

I rested my leg on the scooter and after pushing Hunter back, I was finally able to open the door. The sight of Trace almost made my knees—knee—buckle.

"What are you doing here," I croaked out. Barely containing all the emotions that were flowing through me.

"I heard there was a guy here that might need a little company. Was I wrong?" He said it like he was joking, but the doubt that flashed in his eyes gave him away.

"What are you doing out there, get in here," I said as my voice cracked, and I reached out for his shirt to pull him toward me.

Hunter pushed past me and acted like Trace was an old friend. "Hey, buddy, is this Hunter?" He knelt and scratched Hunter in all his favorite spots, while he acted like Trace was an old friend.

"Hey, traitor," I said to Hunter who ran back in the house followed by Trace. He stood right in front of me and held my face in his hands. *Had it really only been a few weeks?*

"I've missed you so much, Jordan." He took a deep breath and pulled me into his arms. He was trembling, and I knew it wasn't nearly cold enough for it to be from the weather. He buried his nose in my neck, and just held me.

"I missed you too. It feels like it's been so long since I've seen you."

He pulled back and held my arms while his eyes met mine. "We need to talk. There's so much I should have said when you were there. So many things you need to know."

I wasn't sure what he was talking about, but if it meant he'd be here for a few days, we could talk about whatever he wanted. He made sure I was steady on my foot before moving the scooter out of the way. Without a word he scooped me up and carried me to the couch. But he didn't set me down, instead he settled me on his lap and held me close.

Hunter jumped up on the couch next to us and after giving us both a fond look, he took a deep breath and fell asleep. Neither of us said a word for long minutes as we just enjoyed the closeness that we'd both craved for weeks.

"Jordan, I'm not sure I can keep doing the long-distance thing."

"Wait, what are you saying?" I pulled back in his arms and looked for a sign he was joking. But he looked serious, and maybe a little scared.

"I'm saying I want to be with you, I want us to be together not apart. And if that means I have to move here, I'll find a way to do that. I know this probably sounds crazy ... I mean we haven't known each other that long. But I miss you more than I've ever missed anyone. I want more moments like the time we spent at my house. I mean, if that's what you want."

I didn't answer for a moment. Too lost in his eyes and his words that swirled around in my head in such a delicious way I never wanted to end. It took me a second to work out what he had said, and when it finally clicked, his lips were all I wanted. Our lips met and the same heat pulsed through me as it had every time we'd kissed before. "Are you sure? Because I hope you're being serious right now. I miss those nights and days we spent at your house. It feels like it wasn't real, like I dreamed it all."

"It was all real. And what I *feel* is real. I want to make this work."

So many emotions played in his eyes. Some I recognized while others I was afraid to believe were what they appeared to be. I tucked my head under his chin and clung to him. "Stay with me," I whispered.

"There's no place I'd rather be," he murmured, and his lips pressed against my hair.

I soaked up all his warmth, and realized he was right. It was real. My heart swelled with the feelings that continued to wash over me. He was here, it was real.

"Get some sleep, baby, I'm not going anywhere."

As though my body needed his permission, I finally relaxed. After all the weeks of struggling with my leg and feeling like I was driving everyone nuts. Finally, I slept safe in the arms of a man I could so easily love, and if I wasn't mistaken, could possibly feel the exact same about me.

Thirty-Three
Finally, Some Hope

WHILE JORDAN SLEPT, I let my hand trail down his arm, and along his back. If I didn't touch him, I was afraid I'd wake up and all this would have been a dream. It had been a last-minute decision, but if I thought back to the weeks since we'd seen each other, it didn't feel very last-minute at all.

While I was at work, Brad and I had been talking . . .

"You miss him."

"Yeah, is it that obvious?"

"When he was here you were happier than I've ever seen you. And since he left, let's just say you're . . . not."

I pushed off and skied along the top of a ridge checking for unstable snow that could cause trouble for other skiers. Brad skied up to my right and stayed farther away from the edge.

"I'm happy. What's there not to be happy about when I'm living in a beautiful place like this?"

"Look, it's none of my business. But I saw how you two looked at each other that day. There was something between you, and I'm willing to bet if you two had a chance there could be more."

I slid to a stop and lifted my goggles to meet his eyes. "What are you saying, Brad?"

"I'm saying, what the hell are you doing at work when you could be on a flight to Sacramento to see your guy?"

"What?" I was so confused, was he really suggesting I just jump on a plane? The shove he gave me seemed to confirm it.

"Take the day off, buy a ticket, and go see your guy. You're worthless to us here right now. Your heart just isn't in it, and if I had to guess, I'd say your heart is with a guy with a broken leg somewhere in Sacramento."

That was all it took; I skied down to the office and requested a few days off, and as I was walking to my truck, I paid way too much for a ticket on a flight that left that day Today. It had all happened today. I huffed out a laugh and pulled Jordan closer. He stirred but didn't wake, and his dog moved closer and put his head on my leg.

How did I not know he had a dog? Hunter took a deep breath and he was once again out, just like Jordan. Yep, I could do this. We could do this.

◆◆

I awoke to gentle kisses along my jaw, and when I started to smile warm lips were on mine. The same lips I hadn't stopped craving for weeks. "Jordan, I can't believe I'm here."

"So, are you going to tell me what happened that made you decide to be so spontaneous? I mean, not that I mind."

"Well, this morning when Brad and I were out on avalanche patrol, he kicked me in the butt and asked me what the hell I was doing there, when I could be here."

I smiled and played with the hair above his ear. "Remind me to thank Brad."

"Oh, I'm pretty sure I'll be owing him for a while." We both laughed but soon the laughter died down, and we were both left in the comfortable silence we enjoyed.

"What do we do, Trace? I hated the time we were apart, and now that you're here I hate it even more."

"What do you want to do? I'm willing to do whatever it takes to not have to face putting you on a plane by yourself ever again."

"I don't know. I've considered moving to Utah. But I've also considered asking you to move here." His eyes widened, and I wasn't sure if it was shock or excitement. "You're not the only one who's been miserable. If I could have figured out how to get there without having to call you, I would have been there already. I have a few more weeks in this fucking cast and I was hatching a plan to go afterward."

"You were?"

"Don't you dare act shocked, of course I was."

"Jordan, I have to be honest, I don't want to stay away from you anymore. I want us to work something out. That's why I came here. I meant it when I said I'd move here."

"But you love your job, and your house, and your woodshop. I can't take you away from your friends. That wouldn't be fair."

"It's not fair for you to move either. Your life is here. Sorry, I don't want to fight, or stress you out. I just really have missed you so much. We'll work everything out. I know with everything I am that we are meant to be together."

"How long are you here for?" he asked and sat up on the couch but kept my hand in his.

"I work on Monday. I was going to go back Sunday night, but I'd rather get less sleep and go back early Monday. If that's okay—I don't want to mess with your schedule."

"Would it be okay if I flew back with you?"

"Wait, are you kidding? Don't joke with me about that, Jordan."

He cupped my face and brushed his thumb against my cheek. God I'd missed this feeling. "I'm not joking. I can't do much at work, and I'm pretty sure I'm driving them all crazy. Not to mention my mom has to drive me to work. I can ask her to watch Hunter while I'm gone. Is it okay? I mean, do you mind me going?"

"It would make me the happiest man in the world to have more time with you."

He sagged against me. "Oh, thank goodness. I've been trying to find a way to get back to you since I got home."

"Really?" I hoped it was true, but I kept waiting for him to say it wasn't true, and he didn't see a way for us to make it work.

"Really, I think I might be falling in love with you, Mr. Griffin." He froze and turned to slowly meet my eyes. A sweet smile spread on those lips I couldn't get enough of, and I knew right then my heart was his, and it always had been.

Thirty-Four
Working It Out

"Jordan?" my mom yelled into the house as she walked right in without knocking.

"Back here, Mom, give me just a min—" She stepped into the hall just as Trace walked out of the bathroom wearing only a towel. The blush that covered him only made him more attractive. "Mom, geez a little personal space please. This is my friend Trace Griffin. He's the one—"

"—you fell in love with in Utah? Pleased to meet you, Trace, I'm Donna James." She held her hand out, and after shooting me a confused look, he shook her hand.

"Pleased to meet you, ma'am." He shot me another look before rubbing the back of his head and slipping into the bedroom.

"You could have called before you came over," I said as I rushed her into the living room on my scooter.

"I did call, I thought you needed a ride to work?"

"Oh, sorry, Mom. Trace surprised me yesterday and I was so happy to see him, I sort of forgot about everything else."

Her expression softened and she cupped my cheek. "Oh my boy. It's so good to see you happy. I'm sorry I came in hot. I thought maybe you'd slept in."

"It's okay. I talked to Lonny last night and he's fine with me taking some time off. I want to spend more time with Trace so if you don't mind, I'd like to fly back with him and stay a week at least."

"What about Hunter?" she asked, and Hunter's head popped up from where he was asleep on the floor.

"Would you mind?"

"Are you kidding? I miss him whenever he stays here. I think we need to work out a custody agreement." She laughed at that. When I'd brought him home a couple of years ago, she thought it was such a huge mistake to have a dog. But he was such a good boy she couldn't help but love him as much as I did.

I kissed her on the cheek and hugged her. "Thanks, Mom. I really missed him."

"I know, Son. Now you two figure out what you're doing and how you'll make it work. And take your time, as long as Lonny doesn't mind you taking time off. I don't mind looking out for your house and Hunter."

"Ahem," Trace cleared his throat as he walked out of the bedroom. Hair still wet, cheeks flushed, and looking gorgeous.

"Trace, Mom is willing to take care of Hunter and the house while we go back to Utah. We got this." I held my hand out for his and he took it without question.

"Thank you, Mrs. James. I really care about Jordan, and ... well, I really don't want to spend more time away from him."

"You two are adorable! Trace, call me Donna. And you two take as long as you need. We'll all be here when you figure it out." She gave Hunter some loving before saying goodbye and leaving us alone.

"So, I guess this is just the beginning," he said against my lips.

"Seems like it."

He rested his forehead against mine and we stood there soaking each other in until my leg protested, and I needed to sit down.

"So how much longer do you have the cast?"

"I just went for a checkup, the doctor said it's healing nicely, and I can go back to a boot soon. He said depending how I do with it I may not need it for long."

"That's great news. I bet you're more than ready to get rid of it."

"So ready. I had no idea how much of an annoyance a cast could be. You spoiled me. The first few times I showered were not fun. I had a tough time keeping it dry."

"Well you don't have to worry while I'm here. I'll make sure you get plenty of help."

"I know you will. You really do spoil me."

"Good, I want you to know I care. I really care about you."

"I know you do. I care about you too. Probably more than I expected to, but I can't help it."

"I don't want you to try to hide how you feel. I feel it too. Loving you would be so easy."

"Yeah?" I whispered as I met his eyes.

"Yeah. I'm just afraid I'll scare you off and you'll think I'm being too pushy."

"Trace, what if I told you to just go for it. I don't want to hide how I feel either. You've done more for me than I would have ever expected, and I don't want to hide how much that means to me. It's funny, I was beginning to think I might not ever meet someone who I fit with. All it took was Dave leading me down a trail I couldn't handle." His face went from soft to serious in a hot second.

"I still need to have a chat with Dave." His eyes squinted and I didn't want to think about what he was imagining at that moment.

"Trust me, he still feels bad. He's been driving me around whenever my mom can't. And he's tried to help me out at work. Not to mention everyone at work has given him a ration of shit since I got back. They couldn't believe he left me there with you. But then when he told them he hadn't really helped me at the airport, everyone was pissed at him. I think he's paid enough."

He pulled me close again. "Whatever you want, babe. But please promise me you won't be going skiing alone with him again."

"I promise. Pretty sure I won't be skiing anytime soon anyway."

"I'd say this time next year. Maybe sooner."

"Yeah?"

"Yeah." He smiled at our exchange and breathed out my name. "Can we go back to bed now?"

I nodded, and without another word he scooped me up. "I missed you so much."

He didn't answer just smiled at me, and when I smiled back, he kissed me softly. "Those dimples. They get me every time." He walked right into my bedroom, and set me on the bed.

"Want to watch a movie?"

"Sure, I might need to put a TV in my bedroom, this is nice."

"Don't you dare. I love your place just as it is."

"Good thing, because I like it much better with you there."

The thoughts coursing through my mind should have scared me, but they didn't. With Trace, I knew everything would be okay.

Thirty-Five
First Snow

Winter turned to spring, and soon spring turned to summer, and through it all, so much had changed. We'd worked out a routine that everyone around us thought was crazy, but to us it made sense. We took turns flying back and forth every other week. Sometimes it was longer, but it was hard on both of us to be apart too long.

"Dave, what's going on?" Yep, I'd put everything behind me and forgave Dave. If he hadn't been so stupid, I wouldn't have met the love of my life, and for that I owed him.

"Hey, Trace, not much. Are you taking Jordan to lunch?"

"Yeah, we're flying back to Utah tomorrow for a week."

"Nice, how's it working for you two going back and forth?"

"It's not bad. I don't know how it'll be in the winter. My schedule is pretty flexible now but after the first snow I'll need to be there more often."

"Why doesn't Jordan just move there? He could get a job at one of the ski resorts as a mechanic, or if that didn't work there's plenty of auto repair shops."

"I don't know if he's ready for that. He loves working with everyone here, and his family's here."

"Dude, he'd be happy wherever you are. Do you not realize how happy he is since you two met?"

One thing about Dave, he did not hold back. If he had an opinion on something, he told you. And I appreciated that rare honestly. He didn't tell you what he thought you wanted to hear. He told you what his truth was every day.

"I really want us to live together. I hate when we're apart. And I have to admit I love having a dog around."

"Hunter? Yeah he's a great dog."

Another thing about Dave, it was easy to distract him with something else. But not this time.

"Really, Trace, ask him. I've known Jordan for years. And I've never seen him so happy. Plus, if he moves in with you then I have a sure thing when I go there to ski."

"You're not staying at my place, dude." I gave him a stern look then a playful shove. "You can stay whenever you're in town. Though Jordan and I need to rearrange so we have a little more privacy when someone stays. Otherwise we can look over the end of the bed and watch you sleeping on the couch."

"Thanks, I appreciate it." He took a deep breath and scratched the back of his neck with his grease-stained hands. "So, what's your plan, Trace? I know you want him to move in with you. But are you just going to throw it out there, or hope he just doesn't go home one week?"

"I have no clue. I'm not really very good at big gestures."

"Well, I might just have an idea, but it'll take some doing. And we'll have to plan it with the snow. Because for it to work the resorts will have to be open."

"O-kay. I'm afraid to ask exactly what this plan is. But I got nothing else so I guess I'll go with it."

"Leave it to me, you figure out what you're going to say, and I'll make sure you have the perfect backdrop for it." He patted me on the back and walked away just as Jordan walked over to me.

"Hey, everything okay?" Jordan asked, and I leaned in for a kiss.

"Everything's great. What sounds good for lunch?"

"I'm thinking a chicken quesadilla."

"That place on Fourth?"

"You know it. Come on, let's hurry so we miss the lunch crowd."

◆◆

A few hours later I was hanging out at Jordan's house waiting for him to get home so we could go to a movie at the Tower Theatre. It was a retro style theatre that both of us loved and we made sure to visit every time I was in town.

A knock at the door interrupted my random thoughts and I opened the door to Donna.

"Hey, Trace, how's everything going?"

"It's good—oh come on in. Sorry." I was still nervous around her, even though she always made an effort to include me and was always very sweet. "What's going on?"

"Not much." Hunter plodded over to her to say hello before returning to the couch. "Actually, Trace, I wanted to talk to you."

"Oh? About what?" My voice sounded weird even to my ears. I cleared my throat and tried again. "What can I help you with?"

She walked over and sat next to Hunter and played with his silky ears while she prepared to speak.

"Trace, you've made Jordan so happy. I'm just wondering what your plan is? I know you can't continue to go back and forth forever. Once it snows it'll make it even tougher. So, what's the plan?"

"Wow, you're the second person who's asked me that today." I dragged my hand through my hair.

"I'm not asking you for a proposal. I just want you to start thinking about what you'll do."

"I know what I want. I want him to come and live with me in Utah. There's room for him and Hunter. And he could get a job at the resort or one of the auto shops around town. I'm not gonna lie, every time we're apart it gets harder and harder."

"Well if you're waiting to ask him because you're afraid of his answer, don't be. He loves you as much as you love him. It's written all over your faces, and I couldn't be happier. I'll miss having him right here. But I wouldn't mind a trip to Utah now and then."

"What about Mr. James?"

"George? Oh, he'd love to go. He's happy to travel pretty much anywhere. We used to ski years ago. Maybe it's time we try again."

I sagged in relief. It was so good to know we had everyone cheering for us. Now I just had to talk to Dave and see what his plan was.

◆◆

We spent months working it out, waiting for the perfect day. Finally, winter was upon us.

"Babe, I'm sorry but I need to go back today. They're expecting a lot of snow over the next week and they want us all there to start the season."

"Oh, okay. I guess I'll plan to fly out at the end of the week. What do you think?"

"Wait until I see how work looks. I don't want you to fly out and end up spending all weekend by yourself. I'm sorry."

This shit better work out. Because right now I was having a hard as hell time not confessing everything to Jordan and saying fuck it. But then I remembered all the planning, and how much work we'd put into this. And I tried to relax and not give myself away.

"It's okay. I'll get to see you soon. If you're not back here next week then I'll be there for sure." He kissed me and I pulled him in close. I really did suck at this. But in the end, it would be worth it. Or I hoped it would anyway.

Thirty-Six
Our Beginning

SOMETHING WAS UP. I could tell every time I caught Trace talking to Dave. And somehow my mom seemed to know more than I did. She had this smile that she couldn't seem to control whenever she was around us. Trace just acted his normal cool self and grinned right back at her.

"You and me, we're going skiing," Dave announced one day at work. The weather had really changed the past few weeks and Trace had to go back to Utah to be ready for the storms that were expected to dump a ton of snow.

"I'm not sure I'm ready to ski yet."

"Yeah you are. Come on, we'll go to Northstar. You love it there. Lots of trails to just cruise."

"I don't know. I think I'll just wait and ski with Trace when he's here, or we can ski at Park City."

"Jordan, I really want to make up for last season. Come on. I'll pay for your lift ticket and buy you lunch."

I thought about it for a second. This was something we tried to do every year. But since I'd broken my leg I hadn't tried yet. Northstar was the perfect choice, lots of easy to moderate runs that were long enough it wasn't boring. Trace would love it. I shook my head and focused back on Dave.

"You're on. But I'm not taking any chances this time. If you want to ski a black diamond run, go for it. But you'll be doing it on your own."

"Woohoo, I can't wait. I'm going to go tell Lonny we won't be here. We'll be in the fresh pow pow." He pumped his fist as he walked away. I shook my head and checked my phone for a text from Trace.

That night when I was at home, I kicked back on my couch and killed time watching television. As soon as my phone rang, I answered.

"Hey, handsome," Trace said, making me smile.

"Hey, how's everything in Utah?"

"Snowy, it would be better if I had my little heater to keep me warm."

"Hey, don't tempt me. Dave made me promise to go ski with him at Northstar. We usually ski the first day of ski season, and he really wants to make it up to me for last year."

"That sounds fun, although I wish I could be there with you."

"I do too. You realize we still haven't skied together? I just hope I can keep up with you." I had no doubt Trace wouldn't put me in any danger. He was so cautious and fully aware of what could happen if you took too many chances while skiing. I'd learned my lesson too—no more following Dave.

"That's right, we'll need to remedy that this year. Don't worry, we'll have plenty of chances."

"I can't wait. I really want to enjoy it and not be terrified like I am when I trust Dave to lead the way."

He laughed at that, and we talked a while longer until I knew we both needed to get some rest, or we'd regret it the next day.

The rest of the week went pretty much the same, I worked and then at night, Trace and I talked, and enjoyed our time together. I hoped we worked out how we could both end up living in the same place. I loved it here, but I'd give it up in a minute if it meant I got to spend every night with Trace.

Memories flashed through my mind. The nights we'd lay naked in front of his fireplace, making love, and talking for hours. I'd told him I loved him there for the first time.

"You're my heart. You're everything I ever wanted, but never knew I needed. I love you, Trace." He'd held my face in his hands and I'd placed my hand over his. The warmth reflected back at me had enveloped me and made me feel safe and cared for. The soft kiss on my lips had made me want more, but he'd had other plans. He'd rested his forehead against mine for a moment before pulling back and meeting my eyes once again.

"Jordan, I love you. I love how I feel when we're together. You make me feel special, and I hope I never make you feel any less than that. I love you."

A text message brought me back from my thoughts.

I'll pick you up in the morning at around seven. Be ready.

Bring me a coffee and a breakfast sandwich. I'll be waiting for you.

Dave didn't send another message. I knew the routine; he'd pull up ready to go but running a few minutes late. I made sure all my gear was ready before I went to bed. But before I fell asleep, I sent a text to Trace.

Love you, can't wait to see you again. Good night xo

I put my phone on the charger and fell asleep before he answered and awoke the next morning to my alarm at the crack of dawn. After grumbling about the cold and taking a shower, I was as ready to go as I could be. My leg ached a bit in the cold but I took some ibuprofen and tried to ignore it.

"Come on, lots of fresh snow waiting for us."

"Alright, let me load up my gear." In less than ten minutes we were on the road. It had to be a record. We chatted on the way up I80 and I was never more thankful for coffee. "Thanks again for getting this for me. It's really cold out, how low is the snow today?"

"Not sure, but we should make it up there before the heavy stuff gets here."

I checked the weather on my phone. Yep a huge storm front was moving in late in the day. "We should have waited, it's going to be bad driving back."

"Eh we'll be fine. Don't worry."

"Famous last words," I grumbled and watched as the snow got deeper and deeper the higher up we went.

A couple of hours later we pulled into the parking lot of Northstar. It was located just outside the town of Truckee where Trace had grown up, and close to Lake Tahoe. It was one of the bigger resorts in the area, but it still had that small resort feel to it. Dave had bought our tickets online, so we both put our skis down, and clicked into the bindings before we hurried up to the lift to take the first run of the season.

"This is great, isn't it?" Dave said as he sat next to me on the lift. The snow was coming down harder now, and the wind had started to pick up.

"Yeah, I always wanted to ski in a blizzard. I might be spending the day in the restaurant." Especially if my leg started bothering me. Skiing in powder was way different than skiing on groomed slopes where I could glide along without much effort.

He didn't say a word, just turned to me and grinned. His gloved hand came up and wiped at his mouth, but he still grinned like there was a joke only he was in on. Weirdo. I sat and enjoyed the silence of the lift, and the slight crinkle of falling snow hitting my ski pants. As we neared the top we lifted the safety bar, and scooted to the edge to get off the lift.

We skied over to the side and tightened our skis and checked our equipment. As I was bent over another skier skied up where we stood.

"How's your leg?"

I stood up and spun around so fast I almost lost my footing. "Trace?" I asked, as he gripped my arm to steady me.

"Who else would it be?"

I looked between him and Dave as they shared a grin. "See you later, man. Have a good run." Dave skied off by himself and carved through the fresh powder without a backwards glance.

"I hope you don't mind, I wanted to surprise you." He leaned in and kissed me. His lips and nose were as cold as mine, and I had to suppress a giggle.

"How long have you been here?"

"Not long, Dave and I planned this a while back. I rented us one of the cabins along the trail. I thought we could ski for a few days, and if you need a break it's not a big deal."

"Really? Trace, that sounds great!"

"That's not all, I wanted to ask you something else." He didn't look as sure about this, so I reached out and squeezed his arm.

"What is it?"

"Jordan, you know I love you. I want to live with you, and Hunter too. Would you move in with me? I can't take being away from you one more night. Please?"

I kissed him then, and I might have leaned on him hard enough that we both tumbled to the ground and sunk into the soft new snow.

"Yes, I can't take it either. I love being with you and I can get a job there."

"I might have talked to the resort and they're looking for a mechanic."

"No way, it must be meant to be." I hugged him closer and we struggled to our feet. Snow was cold when you were lying in it. "I can't believe you did all this."

"Oh, there's more, I might have arranged for us to have dinner delivered later."

"Dessert?"

"You know it."

"I love you, Trace."

"I love you too, now let's see how that leg's doing." He pushed off and made a wide turn in the fresh powder before sliding to a stop and waiting for me. He cared. He cared and he loved me, and he'd never leave me injured on a mountain with no one around. He'd be there for me, always.

I pushed off and followed the path his skis had left. And right then I knew I'd follow him anywhere, and when he didn't feel like leading, I'd lead the way. We were a team. And we were as perfect for each other as fresh powder at a ski resort on a weekday when it wasn't crowded. Perfect.

Epilogue
Finally, Home

"Hey, you guys ready to go?" Dave called up the stairs at our house. Yes, *our* house. A lot had changed the past year, and one very big change was Jordan moving here from Sacramento.

"Almost, give us a minute," Jordan said from the bathroom where he was brushing his teeth. The water turned off and he walked right up and kissed me. "You ready to go?"

I pulled him to me and ground against him. "You sure you wouldn't rather stay home?" I kissed along the side of his neck hoping to tempt him.

"Babe, it's the first ski day of the new year. I want to go, and I'd really like you to join us." Jordan held my face in his hands before kissing me deeply. "And afterward when Dave is at his hotel, I want you to—"

"Hold that thought," I said, and placed my finger on his lips. "If you start talking like that now we won't make it to the first run." He gave me a sly smile before kissing me again.

"You're right. We can save that for later." He turned and jogged down the stairs like he did every day. The first couple of weeks he'd stayed here had been hard on him. He couldn't make it up and down the stairs on his own and even though I didn't mind helping him, I think he got tired of depending on me for so many things. Which led to me flying to Sacramento more often. It was an adjustment, but whatever it took for us to be together was worth it. Through it all I felt like I was the luckiest guy in the world. Jordan was a great guy, and now he was my guy. Well, truth be told, I was his. I knew that for sure when I watched him drive away with Dave that cold morning last year.

There were times he wasn't sure he'd made the right decision; he had given up his life in Sacramento to move here, but I'd never doubted it. I meant what I'd said to him on the side of a mountain in California in the middle of a snowstorm. He was everything to me, and I treasured each and every moment.

"So, you ready to try Deschutes again?" Dave asked, as we walked out the door carrying our skis.

I waited for Jordan's answer, but I knew what it would be before he said a word. "Nope, I'm happy just cruising, but you go right ahead." Dave slapped him on the back good-naturedly as he passed him to go to his rental car.

"Maybe I'll get lucky and meet someone today."

"Maybe," Jordan met my eyes and grinned. "You just never know where you'll meet the love of your life."

We drove over to Park City for a day of skiing. It was a beautiful bright sunny day, with perfect powder from the night before. But not too much powder that would make it tricky to ski.

"What a perfect day," Jordan said, as he looked up at the resort from the parking lot.

"I can't believe you were able to convince Jim to give you the time off."

"Me either, but I'm really glad he did."

"How's it going working at the resort?" Dave asked as he walked up carrying his skis.

"It's good. I still work on a few of their vehicles, but I also work on the snowmobiles, and even some of the lift equipment. And mostly I love that I get to see hot ski patrol guy while I'm working. Sometimes we even get to have lunch."

"Wow, did I mention how glad I am that I don't have to listen to you talk about him all day at work?" Dave said with a raised brow.

"Maybe once or twice," Jordan said as he pulled his ski boots on.

"How's your leg feeling?" I asked, unable to hide my concern.

He stomped his boot and moved his leg back and forth before looking up at me. "Feels good. I can't tell anything was ever wrong."

"Okay well let me—"

"I promise, I'll say something if it hurts at all." He kissed me again and brushed his thumb against my cheek. "This isn't my first-time skiing since I broke my leg."

"I know, sorry." I ducked my head, but he pressed his finger under my chin to meet my eyes.

"Don't ever apologize for caring." I nodded and we gathered all our supplies and stomped toward the resort in our ski boots. "If you want to carry me the rest of the way I wouldn't mind. Walking in ski boots is a bitch." We all laughed at that and stumbled along to the closest ski lift.

"So, Dave, are you going to go try Deschutes?" I asked, as we clicked our boots into the ski bindings and stomped around making sure they were attached.

"Yeah, I think I'll go check out something new, you two go ahead and we can meet up later," Dave said as he looked around at the different skiers in the area. "Who knows, maybe today's the day I meet the love of my life."

Jordan's eyes met mine and we both grinned. "You never know," Jordan said. The three of us waited for the lift and rode up together to the top. From here there were multiple choices to either go back down, or ride another lift up to the more advanced runs. Dave stood there looking in that direction and didn't look as sure as he had at the bottom.

"Dave, you want to stick with us?" Jordan asked.

"No, you guys go ahead."

Jordan slid closer to me as we studied the ski map. "Why don't we take this black run down?" I suggested. I knew he liked to be challenged, but he didn't want to be terrified on a too advanced run.

"Yeah no more double black diamonds for me. I think I'll stick to a nice blue run today. Intermediate sounds perfect."

"Come on, baby, let's cruise it," I said, and leaned in for an icy kiss. His nose was ice cold, so I kissed it too making him laugh. "Jordan, I'm so fucking glad you're here."

"Me too, and just so you know there's no place I'd rather be. You and me, we're the real deal."

"I love you. I think I loved you that very first day when you were drugged up and giving me googoo eyes."

"My hot ski patrol guy. It was that dimple that did me in." He leaned on his ski poles and grinned up at me.

"You told me that when I was trying to help you that day." I laughed at the memory.

"Come on, let's make the most of this beautiful day, and this perfect powder," I said, and pulled my goggles down. "And no black diamonds." He shoved me and we raced each other to the bottom.

THE END

About the Author

BL Maxwell grew up in a small town listening to her grandfather spin tales about his childhood. Later she became an avid reader and after a certain vampire series she became obsessed with fanfiction. She soon discovered Slash fanfiction and later discovered the MM genre and was hooked.

Many years later, she decided to take the plunge and write down some of the stories that seem to run through her head late at night when she's trying to sleep.

BL Maxwell loves to hear from readers who enjoy her stories, so feel free to reach out at any of these links:

Website: https://blmaxwellwriter.com/ (Free book)
Newsletter: https://sendfox.com/blmaxwell
Facebook: https://www.facebook.com/bl.maxwell.35/
Bookbub: https://www.bookbub.com/profile/bl-maxwell
BingeBooks: https://bingebooks.com/profile/blmaxwell

Also By BL Maxwell

Thank you for reading Double Black Diamonds

Preorder Nuts and Bolts Holiday!
https://books2read.com/NutsNBoltsHoliday
Enjoy a FREE copy of A Night To Remember . A short story with Andy and Link from Remember When.

https://books2read.com/u/baDrw8
Enjoy a FREE copy of The Cemetery Tour a Valley Ghosts Short Story.

https://books2read.com/CemeteryTour
It was just a fun Halloween activity until the ghosts showed up.

Jason Thomas has always loved the supernatural, and anything to do with ghosts. But when it comes to going on haunted tours he'd rather not. His boyfriend Wade books a tour for them at the local cemetery before Halloween thinking it would be fun way to get in the mood for the holiday.

Being connected to the other side of the veil, it doesn't take long for Wade to start noticing a few strange happenings. When ghosts from the past show themselves followed by other paranormal events, they both know there is more going on than a haunted cemetery tour.

This is a Valley Ghosts short story and also foretells events that happen in The Things We Lose. #MM Paranormal Romance, #FREE reads, #Ghost Story

Tangled Weeds (Blinding Light Book Three)

https://books2read.com/TangledWeeds

Blinding Light is back on the road! Rory and Liam are even harder to be around than they were before, and Rory's still in love with Kai. Everything's going great, until Glenn, their drummer, has an unfortunate accident and can't play the drums. Lucky for everyone his nephew, Devon is also a drummer.

Devon Grimes has played the drums since he was old enough to hold a stick, but he's never been known for his responsible choices or showing up anywhere on time. After being kicked out of the band he helped form he's relieved when Blinding Light asks him to step in and jumps at the chance. Now if he can just prove that he's not the screw up everyone thinks he is.

Johnny Brown was lead singer in an up-and-coming band until everything imploded on their first tour. Now he's hoping to find new members that he can rebuild his dreams with and hopefully avoid the drama that destroyed the band. He's a fan of Blinding Light and he's more than curious about their new member, but rumors about his past make Johnny wonder if the hot drummer is worth the trouble.

Divided

https://books2read.com/BLDivided

The four Stroud brothers were all born into magic, and when they all come of age their powers will be revealed. It all sounds like a fairytale, but not all magic is good. Their mother embraced the darkness and paid with her life. Finn Stroud was happy working on the family farm until the day his father announced it was time for them all to go out and find their place in the world, and their magic. He and his four brothers knew this was the tradition of the Imagi people who were meant to wield elemental magic, but Finn soon finds how ill prepared he was for the real world.

Alwin travels from town to town using his own brand of magic to get what he can from anyone that crosses his path. His luck runs out and he's left along the side of the road in a rainstorm. Finn offers him shelter and Alwin offers to guide him in the ways of magic, but everything has a price.

A dark fairytale retelling of The Four Clever Brothers.

#mmromance #mmfairytaleromance #mmfairytaleretelling #magicalrealism #gayromance #darkfairytale #darkromance

BETTER TOGETHER Series

Better Together
Chains Required
The First Twelve
The Better Together Boxset

VALLEY GHOSTS Series

Ghost Hunted

Ghost Haunted
Ghost Trapped
Ghost Hexed
Ghost Handled
Ghost Shadow
Haunting Destiny

THE STONE Series

Stone Under Skin
Blood Beneath Stone
Stone Hearts
The Stone Series Box Set

SMALL TOWN CITY series

Remember When
A Night to Remember (Short Story)
Try To Forget
Try To Remember (Short Story)
One Last Chance
Remember Always (Coming Soon)

CONSORTIUM TRILOGY

Burning Addiction
Freezing Aversion
Cold Blood Warm Heart (Short Story)
Melting Darkness

FOUR PACKS Trilogy

The Slow Death
The Ultimate Sacrifice
The Final Salvation

BLINDING LIGHT Series

Blinding Light
Faded Dreams
Just The Right Chord (Short Story)
Tangled Weeds

PM KISSES

Peppermint Mocha Kisses
Sugar and Spice Kisses

Lobster Tales Duology

Green Eyed Boy
Brown Eyed Boy

Spirit Boys Series

Just Another Day At The Morgue (Prequel)
Dead Things
Living With The Dead
Book three Coming SOON)

Foggy Basin Series

Nuts and Bolts
Nuts and Bolts Holiday

STANDALONE

The List
Double Black Diamonds
Ride: The Chance of a Lifetime
Check Yes or No
A Ghost of a Chance
Tutu
Salt & Lime
Amos Ridge
Six Months

Ten or Fifteen Miles
The Snake in the Castle
A Beach Far Away
Just Another Day At The Morgue
A Lot of Snow For Christmas
Divided
Below Deck

COLLECTIONS

Spirits, Teeth and Wings (A Taste of Paranormal Romance)
The Stone Series Boxset
Four Packs Trilogy Collection
Better Together Universe Boxset
Valley Ghosts Boxset 1
Valley Ghosts Boxset 2

Milton Keynes UK
Ingram Content Group UK Ltd.
UKHW030843141124
451205UK00004B/240

9 798227 064042